GW01162498

Waters of Life

Devorah Gittel Cohen

Artwork by Priscilla Williams

Kadosh L'Cha Publishing

theriverofGod@gmail.com

Thank YOU, LORD!

Oh, how Your Will beats within the chambers of my heart! Help me to listen with the passion of Your Spirit. I want to explode like a triumphant, piercingly sweet shofar, proclaiming Your Nourishing Love Song of Truth into the world.

Thank You for imbedding within my soul, in the very roots of my being, the ability to know You. Thank You for keeping my creativity stayed on Your Purposes, for causing me to draw deep waters of true purpose from Your River, for encouraging me to imbibe the rich abundance of peace-filled Life from Your Source. Help me to dream the desires of Your Spirit as Your Rhythm courses through my veins. Help me to slowly and continuously savor the succulence of Your Fruit, to break open, like an oozing, overripe pomegranate, dripping sweetness upon an expectant, but often unsuspecting humanity.

Oh LORD, Thank you for lending me Your friend, Priscilla Williams. You proclaim the songs of heaven through her paintbrush and heart. You shout and whisper love and greatness through her colors and total devotion to You. You lifted me into Your heavens as we discussed visual images. What a gift! And what a gift are Your dear friends, Marina Polic and Vera Polic! Thank You for their great patience with me. Their expertise and inspiration as graphic designers brought forth the beauty inherent in this book.

Thank You for the readers. I pray they have an open heart, to receive all You have to give them through this devotional art book. May their lives ever be changed as they read the words and ponder the images.

Bless You, LORD, for Who You Are, in all You do, through all of us! Amen and amen.

Introduction

God imagined us in His Mind long before we were born. (Ps 139) We were created in His Image. We envision and create because He envisions and creates. It is part of our nature in Him. The Hebrew word for imagination, yetzer/yatzar, literally means "to form or fashion." When we envision Yeshua's Truth for ourselves, we form or fashion our lives in His Image.

When our "yetzering" wanders away from the LORD's purposes, as in the Tower of Babel, we have turmoil. When our imaginations rest securely in the LORD's purposes, upon the way He is forming or fashioning things, we have peace. Isaiah 26:3 says, "You will keep in peaceful peace the one whose imagination remains at rest, because he trusts in You."

Our Bridegroom's Father has called us to His Son's Banqueting Table of Love. (Matt 22:1-14; Matt 25:1-12) May our imaginations rest upon His Desires...

"It's our wedding day," Yeshua cries. I've set the places, prepared the repast. Please come! I am inviting you to dine. Entwine with My Life! Overflow with My Wine! Thrive in My Vine! Be eternally REVIVED! Come, unite with Me! Our union is the culmination of all I designed."

Like a thief in the night, He's taken you by surprise. Your feet are dirty. Your hair is a mess. Your clothes are soiled. "He won't be impressed!" You hear His voice calling and calling to you. "I shouldn't go like this!" But your heart can't rest. "Oh, GOD, what should I do?" Suddenly, your hair intertwines with lace, your feet are washed, a red carpet is laid. You are cloaked in a robe of royal purple and rose, your gown is white, studded with gold. The fulfillment of Revelation 21 and 22 is revealed in you. Yeshua removes your veil and you become His Good News.

"I've always seen you this way. I knew your perfection before your first day. Your clothes came from Heaven. You received them by grace. See My Banqueting Table, My Glory displayed? I've given you everything, including your faith. You've become my Good News. Come, dine on My Name!" "Yes," you say. "Eternity," He answers, "is yours today."

> "THEN I HEARD THE VOICE OF A GREAT MULTITUDE, LIKE THE SOUND OF MANY WATERS AND LIKE THE SOUND OF MIGHTY PEALS OF THUNDER, SAYING, 'HALLELUJAH! FOR THE LORD OUR GOD, THE ALMIGHTY, REIGNS. LET US REJOICE AND BE GLAD AND GIVE THE GLORY TO HIM, FOR THE MARRIAGE OF THE LAMB HAS COME AND HIS WIFE HAS MADE HERSELF READY." (Rev 19:6-7)

> "THE HOLY CITY, NEW JERUSALEM, CAME DOWN OUT OF HEAVEN FROM GOD, PREPARED LIKE A BRIDE BEAUTIFULLY PUT TOGETHER FOR HER HUSBAND. (Rev 21:2) SHE HAD THE GLORY OF GOD, SO THAT HER BRILLIANCE WAS LIKE THAT OF A PRICELESS JEWEL, LIKE A CRYSTAL-CLEAR JASPER." (Rev 21:11)

Imagine a landscape, full to overflowing with the River of Life.

Imagine the power of the River, seeking to pour itself into all who will receive it.

Imagine walking upstream,
*   easily and without resistance,*
*   through the mighty River towards its Source.*

Imagine a tree, a huge tree,
*   with its roots reaching down,*
*   down through the River of Life,*
*   into the ground beneath it,*
*   with its trunk and its massive branches*
*   stretching out on both sides of the bank*
*   pregnant and over laden with fruit.*

Imagine yourself, the sleeper, the dreamer, walking up through this river.

Envision this landscape, this river,
*   full of the fruits of life,*
*   full of the joys of God's Spirit,*
*   full of the wisdom of God's truth,*
*   full of the magnificence of His presence*
*   full of the passionate ways of His righteousness.*

Experience this river,
*   roaring, seeking, devouring, loving,*
*   cascading, demanding, edifying, engulfing,*
*   destroying, caressing, embracing, rebuilding,*

Dive deep into this river as it flows, rapidly and powerfully,
    out of the base of the Tree of Life, circling around the roots of the Tree of Life

Feel the roots of the tree sink deep into the river,
    Feel the roots of the tree drink deeply of the waters of the river,
        Feel the roots bring the waters of the river into the trunk of the tree,
            Feel the roots lift the waters of the river into the expectant leaves
                of the almighty waiting tree

Watch the leaves dance and sing with the joy of God's laughter,
    Watch the leaves dance and sing with God's abundant good pleasure,
        Watch the leaves dance and sing forever and ever
            For God has filled the leaves with His love without measure

Drink deeply, my friend, of these waters of life,
    fill your roots with the truth from the waters of life,
        bring the waters of life, of the Spirit of life, of the Spirit of Love
            into your own branches, into your own leaves,
                and let God's Spirit within you breathe,
                    as God's fruit matures and ripens in you,
                        and you become God's Tree of life, born anew.

*Now your leaves
can provide shelter and shade
from all the troubles and the problems we face.*

*Now your leaves
can provide balm for our wounds,
healing our pain while their beauty renews.*

*Now your leaves
stretch out to the sun,
they nourish your tree with the light of God's love*

*The light of God's love flows down through your leaves,
down through your branches, and down through your trunk,
descending down through your roots, back into God's eternal river of love.*

*Your leaves are now the most important part of your tree
for through their protection, and the solace they bring
the nations can rest, enjoying God's beauty in peace.*

*But it is God's fruit,
my friend, that nourishes us all.
Without its sustenance our faith might fall.*

*So God says dive deep,
dive deeper still,
until you are immersed and totally filled
with the joy of His presence,
the desire for His fruit,
and all you crave are
His waters of truth.*

*Blossom, ripen,
be born anew.
Feel your tree groan and shake with the weight of your fruit.*

*Be nourished by others
and nourishment be,
as we all learn to become Fruit in God's Tree.*

Imagine a landscape

Full to overflowing

With the River of Life

Becoming The One

Let me share with you my dream… My heart is full to overflowing with God's River of Life, welcoming the LORD's Substance into the center of my existence, so that His Spirit courses through my soul with the full power of His Might. All my man-made barricades are removed, so that I'm fully open to the Stream of His Love, of His Grace, having let Him wash all my internal strife away. I am effortlessly and effervescently sharing His Love, His Healing Power, with the world, enjoying people awash in the Joy of His Presence, without any resistance.

Can we dream this dream together?

We can desire the LORD's Sustenance MORE THAN ANYTHING ELSE in life. Enlist the fullness of His Nourishment. Daily. Hourly. Momentarily. Breathe within the Vapor of His Presence. Intentionally engage with Him in everything we do. Then, God's Living Water will overflow the landscape of our lives. We will wade through our days within His Glorious Love, within His Goodness.

God makes each of us an unconditional offer: His River of Life over our parched existence; His Refreshment, which is unimaginably rich and vibrant, over our thirstiness without Him. When we say "Yes", His River impregnates our entire existence with His Love. He waits for us to choose. When we do, He fully responds. Every moment, He desires to give us more of Himself. How much we receive is up to us.

Let us drink from Yeshua's River, worshiping, praying, and meditating on His Word and watching the Kingdom of God's Glory, of His Light, become ours. Nothing could make our Savior happier.

Contemplating The One

At Calvary, Yeshua procured a victory for all mankind, a victory over evil itself, so it could no longer influence us. He became the Promised Land of God's Heavenly Blessings on earth. In the Old Testament, YHWH gave the Israelites victory over the Land He promised them before they entered it. Yet, He required them to physically conquer the territory in order to experience that victory. Without faith in YHWH, they would never have claimed their inheritance and known His gift. We, just like the Israelites, must claim our inheritance to receive its blessings.

The triumph of Calvary, of Redemption, is gifted to us upon our acceptance of Yeshua as LORD and Messiah. As His children, we freely inherit the bounty of His conquest. But, opening the gift and enjoying its rewards require our complete sacrifice. We must die to self in order to truly live. We must choose to love Him above all else in order to be worthy of Him. (Matt 10:37-38) That is how the Promised Land becomes our home.

At both Joshua's battle at Jericho and Gideon's battle against the Midianites, God sovereignly defeated Israel's enemies. As they obeyed and glorified Him, He gave them the land and the conquest. We, too, are triumphant when we obey God and glorify Him. At Calvary, Yeshua gave us our true Promised Land, a victorious bounty of Shalom beyond our comprehension. But unless we fully enter His Rest, obeying and glorifying Him, we can not fully know its blessing of peace.

"HE WHO BELIEVES IN ME, AS THE SCRIPTURE SAID, 'FROM HIS BELLY WILL FLOW RIVERS OF LIVING WATER." (John 7:38)

Imagine the power of the River

Seeking to pour itself

Into all who will receive it

Becoming The One

Sometimes, we create dams to give us control and authority over the flow of God's River in our lives. We build stony embankments against His Love. We erect walls of non-forgiveness against people who have hurt us, or against God Himself. We idolize societal values that make it difficult for us to joyously and freely surrender to God's Ways. We place one stony thought on top of another, creating impenetrable beliefs about God. We forget that our theological beliefs are necessarily inaccurate, because nobody can understand God completely. Our walls, invisible to our own souls, become impermeable.

Except for God…

Thank God, our dams have sluice gates that let the water through. When we say, "Welcome, God!" or "Help!" we automatically open our sluice gates and God's abundance pours into our souls. Then, He begins His transformative work. As His River pours itself into our lives, He restores everything to righteousness. It is then that we become something almost unimaginable. We become one with Yeshua. We become one with His Love.

Dear LORD, Welcome! POWER of the LORD, transform my life with Your Love. Break up my clods of dirt that cause me to reject the current of Your Fellowship. Come into my hidden fortresses, the protected eddies of my soul. Tear down my mountain islands. Tenderize my stones. Recreate me as a vessel for Your Presence. I want to flow with Your Love.

Yeshua's Arms are outstretched, in love, waiting for your invitation. He wants to completely remove your dams. Are you ready? He desires to utterly overtake your life.

Dear LORD, I don't want anything to stand between us. Thank You for flooding my soul with Your Living Water, now and forever. I never again want to protect myself from You. I never again want to minimize Your impact upon my life. I hand You my sluice gates, my sand bags, my dams, anything and everything I could ever use to keep You out. From now on, I choose life completely engulfed in You.

Contemplating The One

Thank God, Hebrews 12:26-28 promises us that the LORD will remove everything that can be shaken, so that what cannot be shaken will remain. The LORD promises to remove our sins, destroying their influence. They will become non-existent, powerless and forgotten. We will become unshakable and pure. In other words, His Spirit will wash away everything from our lives that isn't one with Him. In the midst of the washing, we can hold onto God's Unshakable Kingdom, filled with His Grace and Forgiveness, and reach out to others in love, not holding their sins against them, nor holding our own sins against ourselves. We can help each other, in love, shake loose, not even bothering to remember each other's dust which God is washing away.

"CLEAR THE WAY OF YHWH, MAKE STRAIGHT IN THE DESERT A HIGHWAY FOR OUR GOD, EVERY VALLEY RAISED UP, AND EVERY MOUNTAIN AND HIGH PLACE HUMBLED." (Is 40:3-4)

"I GIVE WATERS IN THE WILDERNESS AND RIVERS IN THE DESERT TO PROVIDE DRINK TO MY CHOSEN PEOPLE. THE PEOPLE WHOM I FORMED FOR MYSELF WILL DECLARE MY PRAISE." (Is 43:20-21)

Imagine walking upstream

Easily and without resistance

Through the mighty River

Towards its Source

Becoming The One

Do you feel complete? No longer simply interested in the River filling your landscape, has God's River become your landscape? Has God's Presence become the only thing that matters to you? The Holy Spirit, birthing itself within you, has become your life. You feel special, like a Bride on her Wedding Day, prepared to spend eternity with her Groom. Your desire is only for your LORD. He is your portion. You have chosen Him extravagantly, with unbending and unrelenting devotion. "Ah," you think. "This is what it means to die to myself. I have chosen life in Messiah. I am happy."

His River is your home. No longer merely drinking His Waters, you are becoming His Waters. You press upstream, towards His Throne, passionately, but with complete ease and relaxation. His River, now your Home, embraces you, making room for you, propelling you towards YHWH, your Source. The LORD's Spirit pierces your core, bringing your guts, your flesh, into His Heart. His waters plummet even deeper. You and God's River, God's Spirit, become one. Your heart plunges into the Father's, encapsulated in His Love. You are undistracted, lost in God's Goodness, unable and unwilling to be diverted, focused on birthing God into your existence.

> Dear Lord, I want to live like this. Help me, please! I only want Your Presence. You are the only thing that matters. Become my life. Let everything else die. Because of my singular focus on You, I will thrive. Amen.

Contemplating The One

The River, God's Spirit, is the flow of God's Love in our lives. Through it, we experience the fullness of YHWH within our own hearts. It is God's gift to us. Coming from His Throne and from Yeshua, we are meant to gift it back to the world. (Jer 2:13, John 7:37-38, Rev 22:1) As it brings us God's fullness, it empowers us to bring His fullness to the nations, so everyone can know Yeshua. (Acts 1,2) Our helper, our advocate, our intercessor, our guide, our teacher is God's Spirit. He is the Truth. (John 14:16-17, 26; Acts 8) Showing us how to love God and each other, He declares to us everything that belongs to the Father, through His Son. (John 16:14-15)

God has chosen to create His Temple on earth through us. Our innermost beings are the location for His Throne. Through groans too deep to understand, God's Spirit lifts our needs up to our Father. Our Father meets our needs by continuously sending His Spirit to fill them. His Throne is a place of help and provision for our souls. God's Spirit, teaching us how to do what our Father says, comforts us when we err, and encourages us. (John 16:13) Through God's Spirit, we become the fulfillment of His Promise.

> Dear LORD, Thank You for the gift of Your Spirit. Thank You, dear Spirit, for all You do for me every moment. I pray that You will change my heart so it can only feel Your Love, can never respond to anything less, and is never attracted to anything else. I ask to be so thoroughly embraced by Your Love that I can only experience You. In Yeshua's Name I pray. Amen.

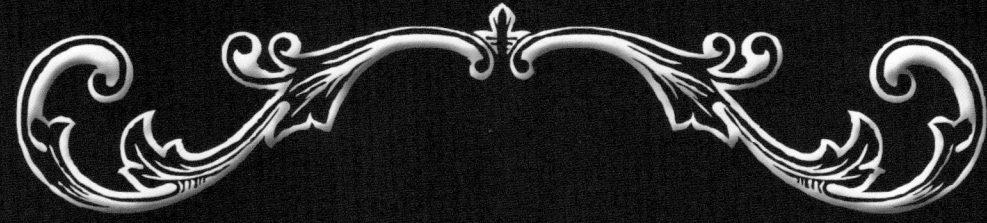

Imagine a tree, a huge tree

With its roots reaching down

Down through the River of Life

Into the ground beneath it

Becoming The One

Out of the River, on both sides of its banks, grows the Tree of Life. It is the final guardian before God's Throne in Revelation 22. It overshadows us with its leaves of healing and fills us with the Fruit of God's Spirit. Rising up from the pith of God's Seed, its roots plunge deep through His Waters of Truth into the Bedrock of His All Consuming Love. Its Fruit, forbidden to us after the Fall, is returned to us after Yeshua. When we eat of its fruit, the Fruit of Life, Yeshua's Redemption courses through our veins, His Blood becomes our blood, and our new DNA escorts us up to God's Throne, to live with our LORD, forever.

Here, the fullness of God dwells. Here, within our hearts, minds and souls, is a place so tender, deep, and pure, it quivers at God's Touch. Here, within His Holy Communion of love and acceptance, our Spirits remain eternally one with our LORD. Beyond sight, beyond understanding, we dwell together with our Father, rooted in the Bedrock of His Creativity. We become His Shalom. Unmovable. Unshakable. Eternal. Still. Our spirits, born in the soil of God's Creation, in existence before Time began, join His Waters. Nourished in the mind of God, trees of life planted by the LORD to glorify His Name, our roots absorb His Compassionate Mercy and press down into the foundational soil of His Grace.

Dear LORD, it is incomprehensibly, unspeakably, wonderful that the fullness of Who You Are dwells within us. Thank You for growing us into Your Tree of Life, for giving us Your Roots of Shalom, Your Roots of Joy. You are our bedrock, our river, our foundation; the Planter of all that is good and worthy within us, and we worship You, O LORD! Have Your Way with us. Amen.

Contemplating The One

The Scripture quotes below are transposed to first person, as a declaration of our commitment to God.

I TRUST IMPLICITLY IN YOU, LORD, FOR YOU ARE MY SECURITY. I AM LIKE A TREE PLANTED NEAR WATER, SPREADING MY ROOTS BY YOUR RIVER. EVEN IN SWELTERING HEAT, IN A DROUGHT, MY FOLIAGE REMAINS RICH, YIELDING FRUIT, AND MY THIRST IS ALWAYS QUENCHED. (Jer 17:7-8) BECAUSE I FULLY BELIEVE IN YOU, I NEVER THIRST. (John 6:35) YOU GIVE FREELY TO ME FROM THE FOUNTAIN OF THE WATER OF LIFE, (Rev 21:6) AND I ALWAYS COME TO YOU BECAUSE I AM ALWAYS THIRSTY FOR YOU. (REV 22:17) BECAUSE I AM ALWAYS THIRSTY, I KEEP COMING TO YOU, YESHUA, AND DRINKING. I BELIEVE IN YOU. LET RIVERS OF LIVING WATER FLOW OUT FROM MY BELLY TO THE WORLD. (John 7:37-39)

Dear LORD, thank You for planting me by Your River, for drawing Your Water into my roots. Thank You for making me beautiful and fruitful. You always give me everything I need. But the thirstier I am for You, the more fully I receive, and the more fully I am satisfied. Thank You for teaching me to trust You completely, so Your River of Life can flow freely into me, and freely from me, into the world. I love You.

With its trunk and its massive branches

Stretching out on both sides of the bank

Pregnant and over laden with fruit

Becoming The One

Although conceived before time, our true identities, our true spirits, were not integrated into us until our resurrection in Yeshua. When we were lost in sin, they were guiding us, pushing us up through the darkness into Messiah's Outstretched Arms, encouraging us to grab ahold of him and never let go. Once we receive new life in Yeshua, they become our internal strength, trunks of righteousness that suck up God's Waters of Grace into our souls and bodies. Never tainted, always pure, they know God to the very core of their beings. Beacons of His Light that brought us Home, they grow strong and straight, drinking lavishly of YHWH's Wisdom, pushing us up into His heavens, declaring His Goodness every moment of every day.

God's Spirit blows in our leaves. God's multi-colored, multi-dimensional Ray of Light penetrates the moments of our days. God's Synthesis revives our senses, bringing health to our frames. God's Fruit, the sweet fragrance of His Love, invigorates our hearts with its intoxicating, increasingly nourishing aroma of Holiness. We touch His Fruit's soft skin, taste its rich nectar, chew on its delicious flesh, swallow its life giving strength, the influence of His Seed pressing down and shaking our hearts. We burst forth with His Love as we mature. Joy, Patience, Kindness, Goodness, Faithfulness, Meekness, Self Control and Righteousness are what we become. Declaring the heart of God's Goodness, we nourish, satisfy and stimulate people's appetite for the LORD.

Contemplating The One

IT PLEASED THE FATHER TO HAVE HIS FULL BEING DWELL IN HIS SON, AND THROUGH HIM TO RECONCILE ALL THINGS TO HIMSELF. (Col 1:19-20) HE PUT ALL THINGS UNDER HIS FEET, AND MADE HIM HEAD OVER ALL THINGS FOR THE CHURCH, WHICH IS HIS BODY, THE FULLNESS OF HIM WHO FILLS ALL IN ALL. (Eph 1:22-23)

Think carefully on those scriptures. Think carefully of Who God Is. Can we imagine that in Messiah Yeshua, God the Father's FULLNESS dwells within us? That we, the church, are Messiah's Fullness? That we, personally, are an expression of Messiah's Fullness? Since God's fullness is absolutely infinite and limitless, since Yeshua's Fullness dwells within us, we, His church, are absolutely infinite and limitless. Through Him, we too are good beyond measure.

God's Word does not lie, nor come back void. This is YHWH's Truth. By learning to abide ever more fully in Messiah's Love, believing in His Words, we can discover YHWH's Meaning. God will bring His Word ever more strongly into our lives. Choosing to be who we are in Messiah, we can apprehend YHWH's Covenant with us. Doing this on our own, we will utterly fail. Hubris, selfish pride, and heaps of trouble will be the result. But if we intentionally welcome God's Victory, looking for its evidence, He will magnify Himself within us and we will see His fruit. Yeshua said, "HE WHO ABIDES IN ME AND I IN HIM BEARS MUCH FRUIT. APART FROM ME, YOU CAN DO NOTHING." (John 15:5)

Dear Yeshua, You said, "Because I live, you also will live… YOU WILL KNOW THAT I AM IN MY FATHER, AND YOU IN ME, AND I IN YOU." (John 14:19-20) Thank You!

Imagine yourself

The sleeper, the dreamer

Walking up through this river

Becoming The One

How it pleases YHWH to transform and bless us while we sleep! As we dream we work out the unspoken yearnings of our hearts, and our souls express their hidden desires and their deepest longings. When we give YHWH our sleep, our times of rest become peace-filled, healing adventures, times to experience the full extent of God's Powerful Loving Transforming Glory. He delights in our encouragement and our agreement. He awaits our request for full restoration with bated breath…

Dear LORD, thank YOU for the holiness You invest in me at night. Thank You for Your glorious night visions that bathe my days in Kingdom Wonder. Thank you for ripping apart everything in me that does not serve You, rearranging me according to Your Purposes. Thank You for sleep, a time for You to restructure me without my need to think or function. Thank You, LORD GOD, for You. Make me ready for Your work. Amen.

Contemplating The One

The Hebrew day begins at sunset. Day is birthed from night, fetuses conceived in dark wombs. God hovered over unformed darkness like a mother. His Creative Power delights in creating order out of chaos, light out of darkness. God breathes dreams into hearts to establish and grow His Order, which demonstrates His Kingdom. Think of Jacob and his ladder and Daniel and his visions. Think of Joseph from the Old Testament and Joseph from the New. Prophetic dreams bring us glorious experiences of God's Provision, leaving us exulted or terrifyingly awestruck. They give us direction. Teaching dreams give us greater understanding of God's Reality. They exhort us. Healing dreams restore us to God's Kingdom, leading us past our wounds and challenges, physical, emotional, mental and spiritual, and restoring us to peace, shalom, and wholeness.

God often provoked destiny in our Biblical ancestors through dreams, causing revolutionary, soul and earth shaking, changes. For instance, He caused an ecstatic trance to fall upon Adam when He created Eve, (Gen 2:21) and He caused a similar trance to fall upon Abraham when He covenanted with him. (Gen 15:12) God also uses dreams to expand His Kingdom. Pharaoh's God-given warning dreams resulted in Joseph saving the Middle East from famine, which introduced the entire area to God. (Gen 41:57) After Nebuchadnezzar's prophetic dreams came to fruition, the king declared YHWH Lord of his empire. (Dan 4:34-37) Peter's trance vision provoked him to bring the Gospel to the nations. (Acts 10)

"IN A DREAM, A VISION OF THE NIGHT, WHEN A TRANCE FALLS ON MEN WHILE THEY SLUMBER IN THEIR BEDS, THEN HE OPENS THE EARS OF MEN AND SEALS THEIR INSTRUCTION, TO TURN MAN FROM HIS DOINGS AND HIDE MAN FROM PRIDE."
(Job 33:14-18)

Dear LORD, I sleep, submitted to Your Will. Come, freely birth Yourself within me. Bring Your Destiny upon me and inspire me, I pray, as I sleep. Remove any dreams or desires that do not please You, and bless those that serve You. May my days grow Your Kingdom, and may my nights prepare me to do so. As I rest, turn my jagged, wounded hardness into Your Gracious, Loving Wholeness, so I may more fully reveal You to the world. Amen.

Envision this landscape

Full of the fruits of life

Full of the joys of God's Spirit

Full of the wisdom of God's Truth

Full of the magnificence of His Presence

Full of the passionate ways

Of His Righteousness

Becoming The One

When we spend all our moments envisioning the LORD's Presence, we will experience the continuity of His Peaceful Peace. (Is 26:3)

> So, let us… *CHOOSE* to let His River flow through us without any obstructions from our minds, hearts and souls. *DECIDE* to experience His Joy, Wisdom, Spirit, Truth and Magnificent Presence. *DETERMINE* to stay focused on His Love. Then, we will be filled with the compassionate ways of His Righteous Love, for His Righteousness is Love.

His Fruit is love. His roots are love. His trunk is love. In Him, we are love. He produces nothing else. A good tree bears good fruit, and God is Good, wonderfully, eternally, forever GOOD. His Heart in our hearts, His Life in our lives, His Soul in our souls, His Spirit in our spirits, is good. The roots of His Joy, Wisdom, Presence and Righteousness are producing His Righteous Love, His Good Fruit, within us. Selah.

> So, let us… *STOP and do nothing. RELAX into His Spirit, into His Love. LET HIM reform us, re-imagine us, into Himself. He's doing it today, right now. Whether He's bringing up dross, or polishing silver, He's refashioning us into Himself. He's refashioning us into Love. He's envisioning us, right now, as His joyous, wise, magnificent, righteous, love.*

> *Dear LORD, I ask to become Your Love. May the victory of Your Love be completely revealed in me. Help me to always envision Your Blessings spilling over from my heart. Help me to overflow with Your Grace. I cannot carry Your Love through my own efforts. But through Your Spirit, which dwells fully within me, Your yoke is easy and Your burden is light. I can do all things through YOU! (Matt 11:30 and Phil 4:13)*

Contemplating The One

In Matthew 13:33 and Luke 13:21, Yeshua compared the Kingdom of God to yeast that leavens a woman's batch of dough. When yeast is kneaded into a batch of dough, the yeast will eventually leaven the entire batch. The yeast is Yeshua's Spirit on earth, eventually transforming all of existence into the expansiveness of Heaven. As Yeshua's Fullness, we are that leaven. As people, we are also the dough being transformed by that leaven. Although the process of transformation can hurt, if we identify with the finished product, the process of transformation becomes a joy. We can sense, moment by moment, that we are becoming what we were meant to be forever, children of God, living embodiments of God's Magnificence.

The Hebrew word for "imagine" comes from the word for "form." (Strong's H3335, H3336) Every moment of every day we are forming our thoughts. Every moment of every day we are envisioning the world we experience. It's impossible to stop the process. The way we form our thoughts determines how we experience our lives. But it is possible to harness the process. If we form our thoughts around God's Holiness, we imagine a world completely informed by God's Sanctity. If we form our thoughts around God's Love, we imagine a world completely filled with God's Blessings. God formed or imagined us to bless the world with Him. He created us to be His living Emissaries of Shalom. (Matt 28:18-19)

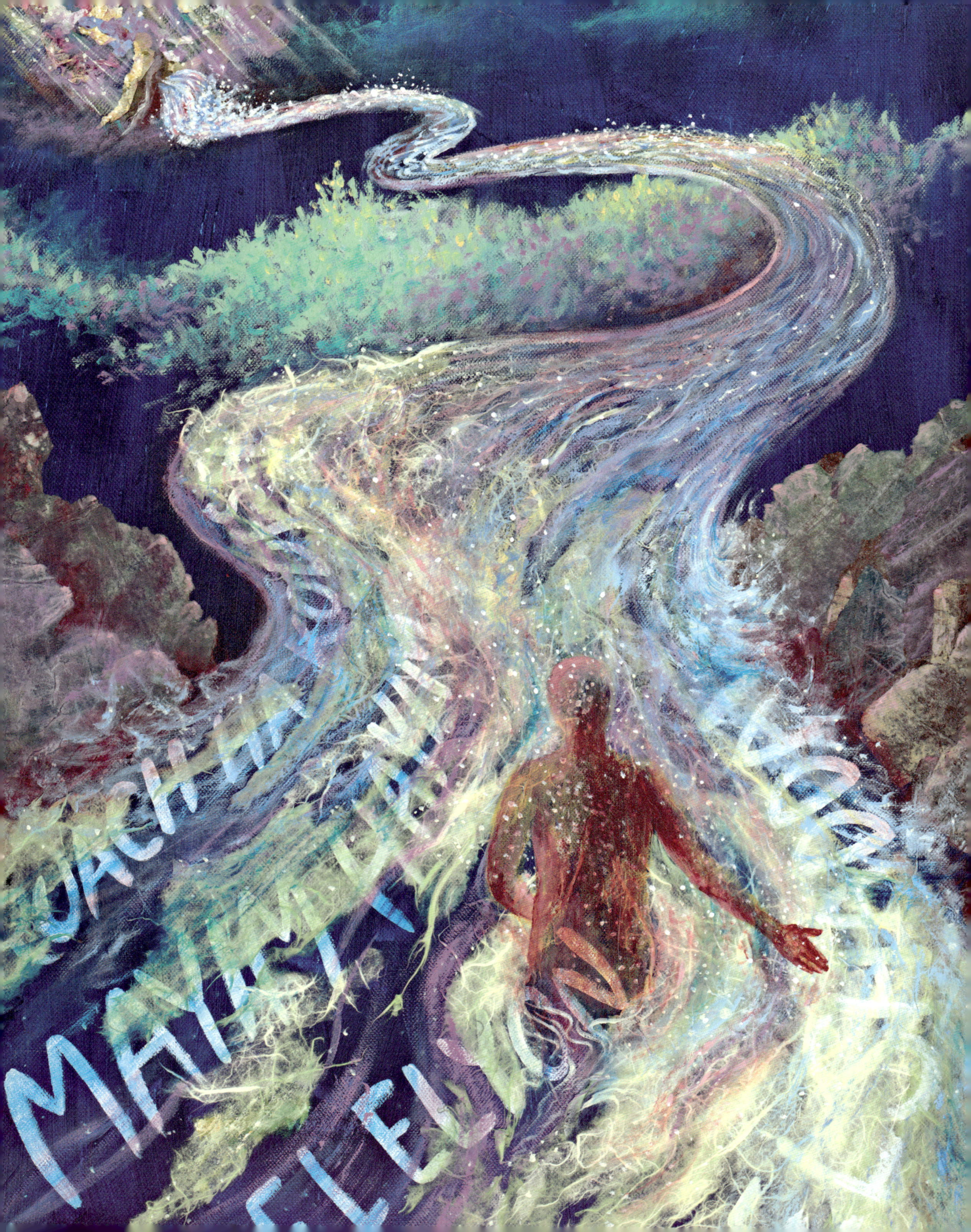

Experience the river

Roaring seeking, devouring, loving

Cascading, demanding, edifying, engulfing

Destroying, caressing

Embracing, rebuilding

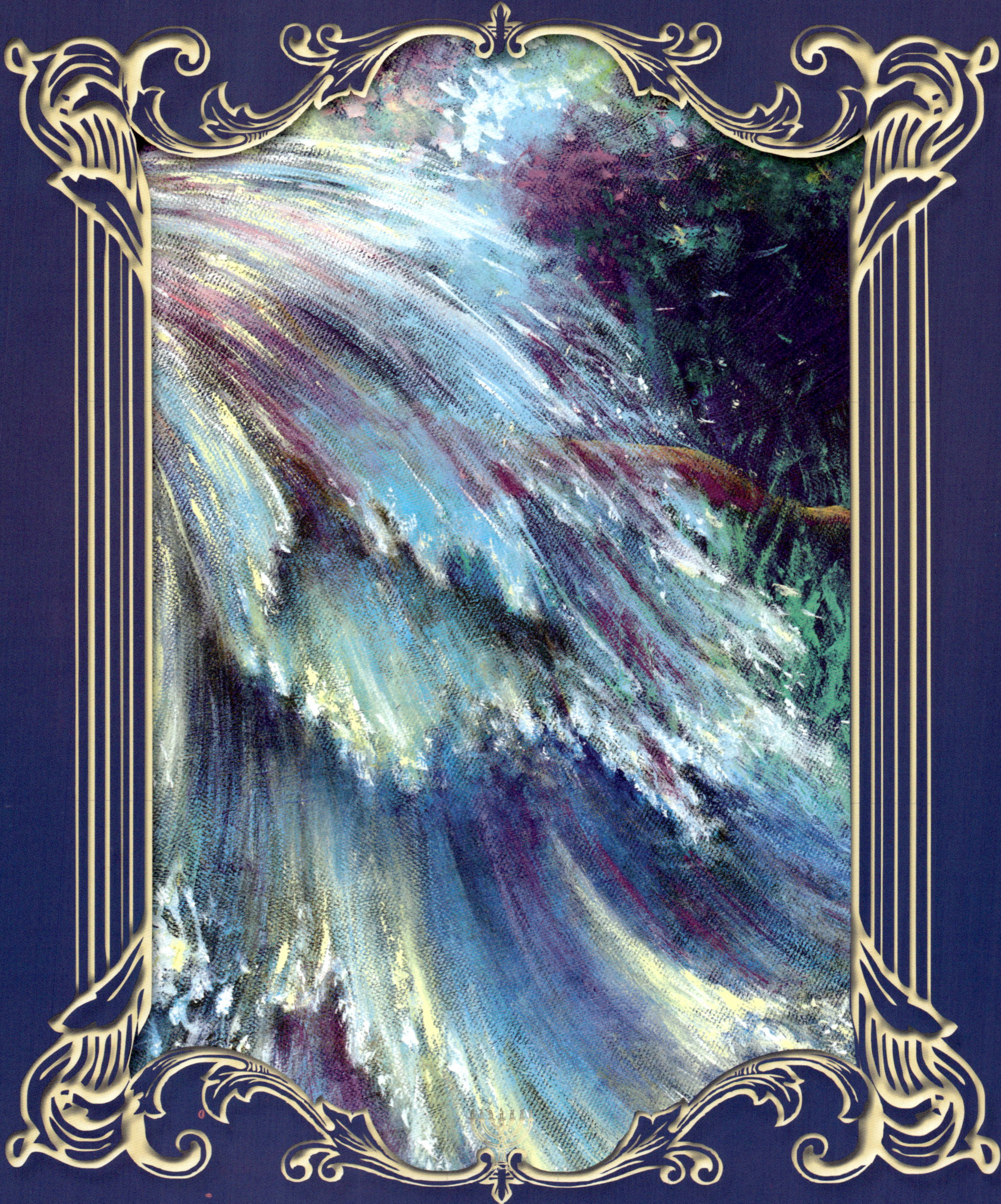

Becoming The One

Press on, surrendering detail after detail of your life, opening yourself to holy desire after holy desire, as God's River roars its Sanctity into your flesh. Invite Him to plunder your sin and selfish pride, devouring your lies and messes with His Awesome Purity and Humility. He is provoking you into perfect unity. Let Him cascade into your self-protection, gushing into your hidden quivering frailty with His peace. Invite Him, your soul's sole protector, to demand that you use your God-given faith to trust and worship Him. Let Him edify your limited, self-occupied mind with His Endless, Eternal, Incomprehensible Righteousness, Wisdom and Compassion. Invite Him to engulf your self-focused darkness with His Heavenly/Globally focused Light. Let Him destroy your hungry, needy identity with His satiating, filling Love, bursting your dams of deprivation with His fullness of satisfaction. As He embraces you with His Compassion, His Joy becomes yours, His Vision, yours, His Reality, yours. Invite Him into all your strengths and weaknesses. Seek complete and total union with Him. He will rebuild you, fully and utterly, into Himself. And you will understand, finally, who you are, because you are His Creation.

> "BEHOLD, I STAND AT THE DOOR AND KNOCK; IF ANYONE HEARS MY VOICE AND OPENS THE DOOR, I WILL COME IN TO HIM AND WILL DINE WITH HIM, AND HE WITH ME. HE WHO OVERCOMES, I WILL GRANT TO HIM TO SIT DOWN WITH ME ON MY THRONE, AS I ALSO OVERCAME AND SAT DOWN WITH MY FATHER ON HIS THRONE." (Rev 3:20-21)

Contemplating The One

YHWH exists because He exists. But perhaps, in some way we cannot understand, He exists for love, because He is Love. And perhaps, because we were created in His Image, we exist for love. We only know true life to the extent we love. Our existence depends upon love. God zealously, continuously loves us and we were created to zealously, continuously love Him. Yeshua loves us beyond compare. He gives us everything. Can we love Him the same way? Beyond compare, giving Him everything? When Yeshua is the center of our attention, when we focus on nothing less, our relationship with Him has no limitations or restrictions. We serve Him in ways that seem unimaginably wonderful. He heals the tug of war on our souls, giving us everything we need to pursue Him, everything we need to be protected, everything we need to be loved, and everything we need to be filled with His Joy.

> "'YOU SHALL LOVE THE LORD YOUR GOD WITH ALL YOUR HEART, AND WITH ALL YOUR SOUL, AND WITH ALL YOUR MIND.' THIS IS THE GREAT AND FOREMOST COMMANDMENT. THE SECOND IS LIKE IT, 'YOU SHALL LOVE YOUR NEIGHBOR AS YOURSELF.' ON THESE TWO COMMANDMENTS DEPEND THE WHOLE LAW AND THE PROPHETS." (Matt 22:37-40)

Dear LORD, just as the Law and the Prophets are completed by love, may my entire life be completed in Your Love. May I become Your Love. May I only know Your Love. May I become Love's Destiny. Shalom.

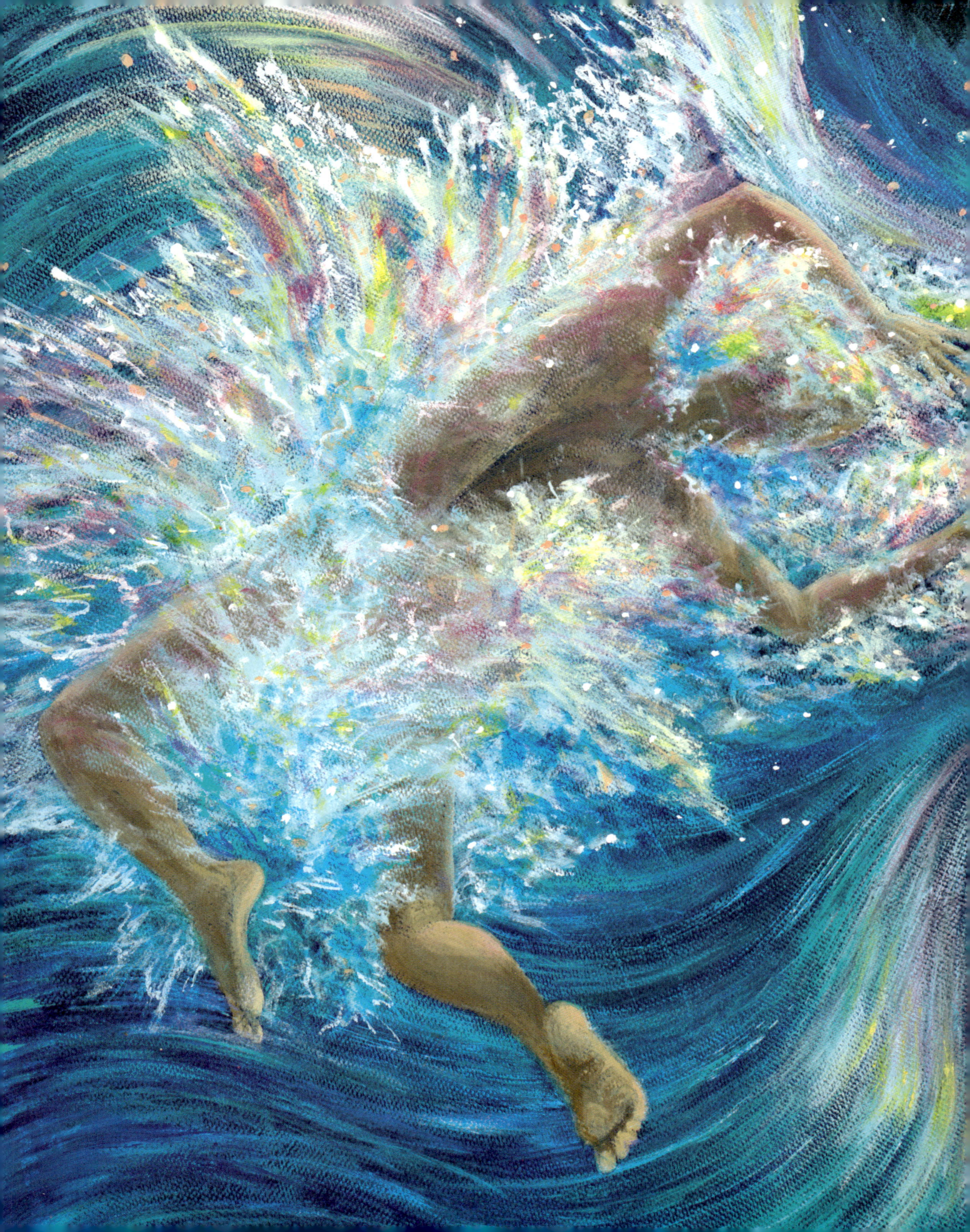

Dive deep into this river

As it flows, rapidly and powerfully

Out of the base of the Tree of Life

Circling around the roots

Of the Tree of Life

42

Becoming The One

Drink from Yeshua like a baby drinks from its mother. *Rest.* Feed from Him like a baby feeds from his mother. *Trust.* Let your hearts beat together as one. *Tremble.* Become one with His Heartbeat. *Shake.* Become one with His amazing love. *Laugh.* Let the fearsomeness of what you are doing, of what He is doing, grab ahold of you. *Shudder.* In His Heartbeat is Utter Holiness. *Fall at His Feet.* Invite Him into your foundation. *Quake.* Come into intimate, complete communion with a God who destroys everything that does not glorify Him. *Die.* Resurrect as a vessel for the Victory He accomplished upon the Cross. *Live.*

Nothing is required of you except your childlike faith. *Wait.* He accomplished everything upon the Cross, the most carnal expression of God's unending love for you. *Breathe.* Pick up your cross. *Do.* Fall on the cornerstone of your faith. *Repent.* Let the Glory of God be revealed within you. *Surrender.* Collapse into Him and be restored into His Holiness. *Be.*

According to Isaiah 28:16, "He who believes (in the cornerstone) will not '"chush,"' (H2363). Say "chush" quickly and repeatedly out-loud. Doesn't it sound like rushing? It means physical, emotional or mental hurry. We cannot trust in our Cornerstone Messiah and blow around chaotically, whirlwinds of panicked excitement and mental turmoil, manipulating life to succeed or survive. Instead, we need to stay faithfully calm, resting in our LORD in joy and wonder. He will do His excellent work. He will take care to rebuild us into His Perfect Image.

Contemplating The One

People become frenetic when they try to cover up the evidence of their actions and beliefs. They are simply covering up sin with a fig leaf. Isaiah 28:17-21 says they are covenanting with death, and God vows to cover up those deadly covenants with searing destruction. Isaiah describes this cleansing work as "strange" and "alien." Foreign gods and non-Israelites, in Scripture, are "strange" and "alien." Only here, in Isaiah 28:21, do those words (H2114, H5237) apply to God's work. Why? Check out 1 Peter 2:1-16. There, quoting much of Isaiah 28, Peter says that we, who used to be foreigners to God, are now "strangers" and "aliens" to the world. We are God's Priests, who, in our goodness, abstain from earthly passions. We even treat our persecutors well, causing them to glorify the LORD. Thus, we are God's "strange and alien" work. Through us, He reveals the peculiar truth of people whose lives are completely sacrificed to Him, of people who use their freedom to only do His Perfect Will. That's because Yeshua's "strange and alien" work upon the cross ended our covenant with death. Because of Yeshua, we dwell upon God's foundation of eternal life. When we drink from Yeshua, we never "chush," we never need to cover up our mistakes, and we never need to run from our persecutors. We remain expressions of God's Goodness and Love, living into eternity in His Shalom.

> *Dear LORD, I love You more than life itself. My Best Friend, may internal fellowship in Your Blood, in Your Life, cause me to remain a stranger forever to all that is alien to You. Thank You for Your utter rest. Amen.*

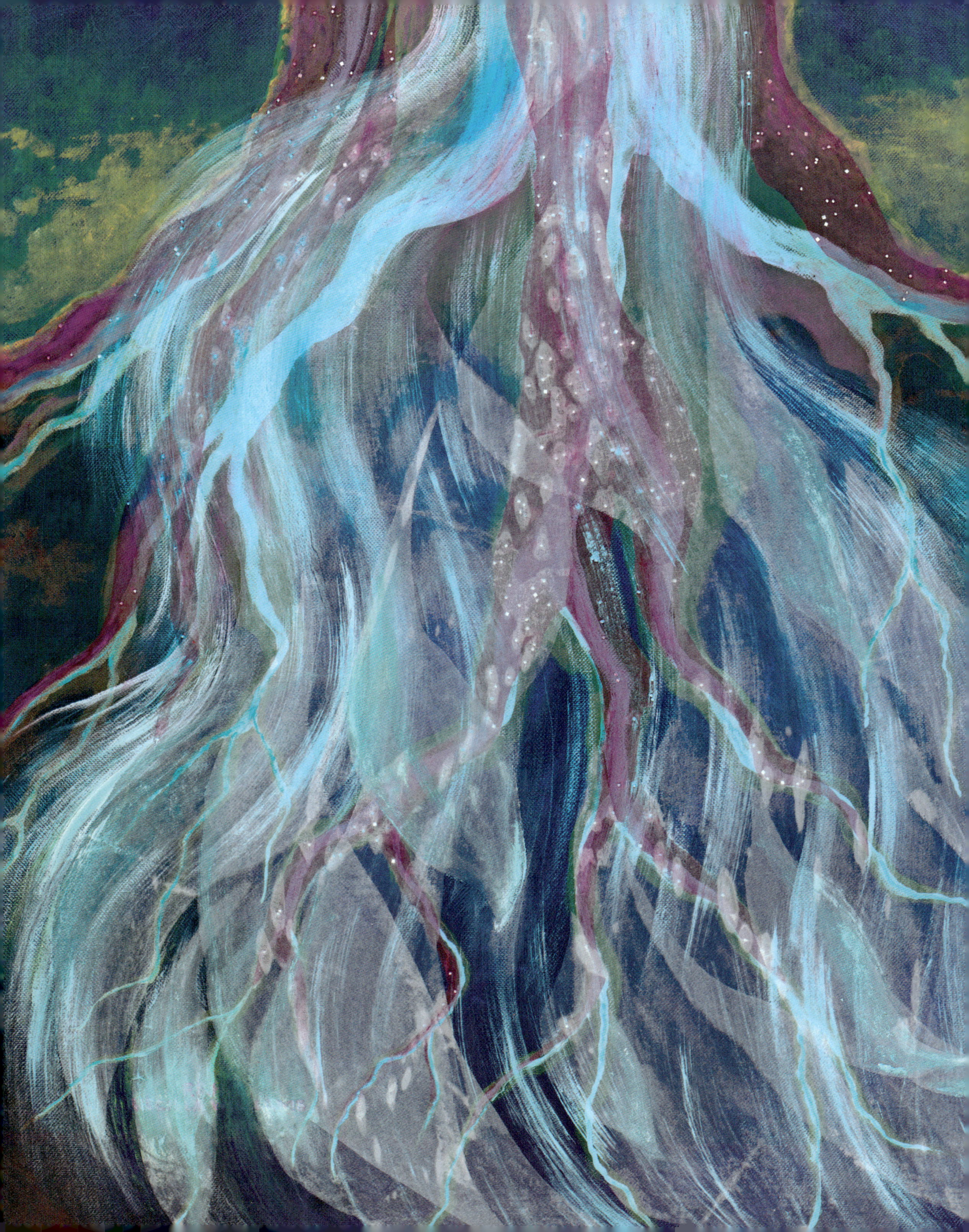

Feel the roots of the tree sink deep into the river

Feel the roots drink deeply of the waters of the river

Feel the roots bring the waters of the river

Into the trunk of the tree

Feel the roots lift the waters of the river

Into the expectant leaves

Of the Almighty waiting tree

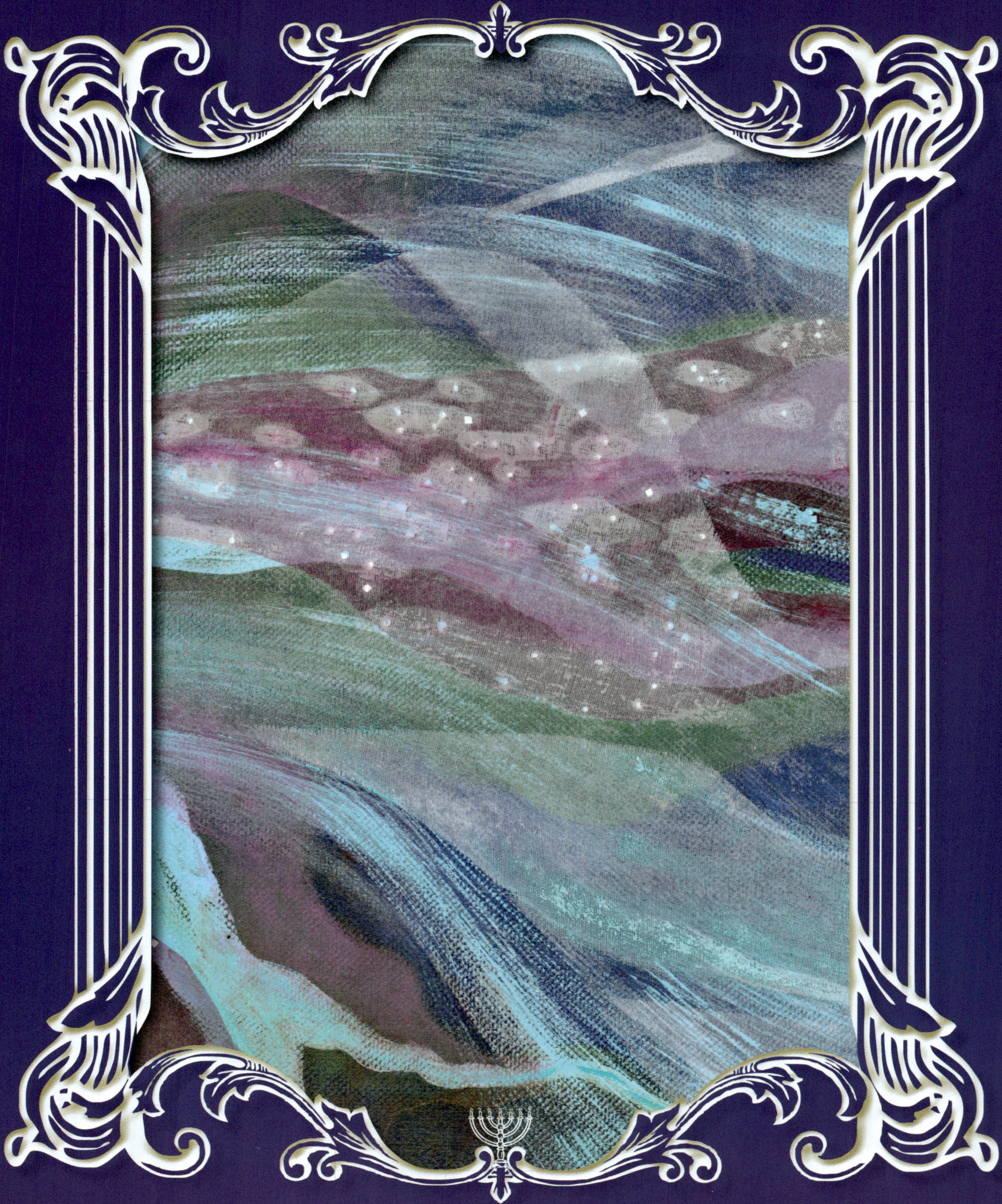

Becoming The One

Dear LORD, You are my heart's desire! Where nothing exists except Your Love, the fullness of Your Shalom dwells. Where everything else is surrendered to You, only the completion of Your Provision remains. I choose this. I choose to live and breathe and eat and dance and sing and worship and rejoice only for You, so only You exist within me and all of me exists within You.

Out of the roots, out of the guts of my soul, I desire Your Transforming Power. Out of the base of my being, out of the deepest core of my existence, I yearn for Your Joy, Your Delight and Your Freedom. May they bubble up within me with abandon! I choose to BE and not to worry, to celebrate and not to struggle, to love and not to begrudge. I rejoice in the truth that You are in charge. I will have no fear. I will live each moment within Your Grace. People will see You on my face. You will touch their souls, commiserating and celebrating with them through me. Your Compassion will fill me to overflowing. Your Goodness will become my completion. I am nothing in and of myself, but in You, I am one.

Contemplating The One

Rest is the price of this intimacy with God. Shalom is the currency of this celebration. When we are at rest in Yeshua, drinking of His River, we become wells of water springing up to eternal life. (John 4:14) When we are at rest in Him, imbibing His truth, from our innermost beings flow rivers of Living Water. (John 7:38) We become heavy with His Presence, compelled to relieve ourselves of His burden, of His weight, of His glory, compelled to give away what we can no longer contain. When we are at rest in His Presence, He does this. Without our doing it, He heals the world through us.

> So, let us... *Be humbled to silence, internal silence. Wait upon Him, each and every second, awestruck, arms raised, fingers one with the beckoning reach of His Almighty Waiting Tree. Encourage His Waters to pour into us and out of us till we cannot contain them. Watch His Tree of Blessing, His Tree of Love, break the shackles of the world through us. Dance in His Pleasure as He rejoices through us, His Blessing, His Goodness, His Good Fruit, His Shalom, becoming ours. Give Him to the world, so He can heal the world through our holy submission. Touch the world with His expectant, effective leaves of healing.*

It is only God who gives us this true shalom. (Num 6:26) He gives us the Prince of Shalom. (Is 9:6) He gives us possession of the earth when we are meek. Then, He pampers us with great shalom. (Ps 37:11; Matt 5:5) When we trust in Him, we do not fret or get angry at evildoers. Instead, we rest quietly before Him, dancing and praising Him with all our might. As He fulfills the desires of our hearts, we behave righteously. Thus, our finish in Him is His Shalom. (Ps 37:1, 3-4, 7, 37) On the cross, Yeshua said, "It is finished." Shalom.

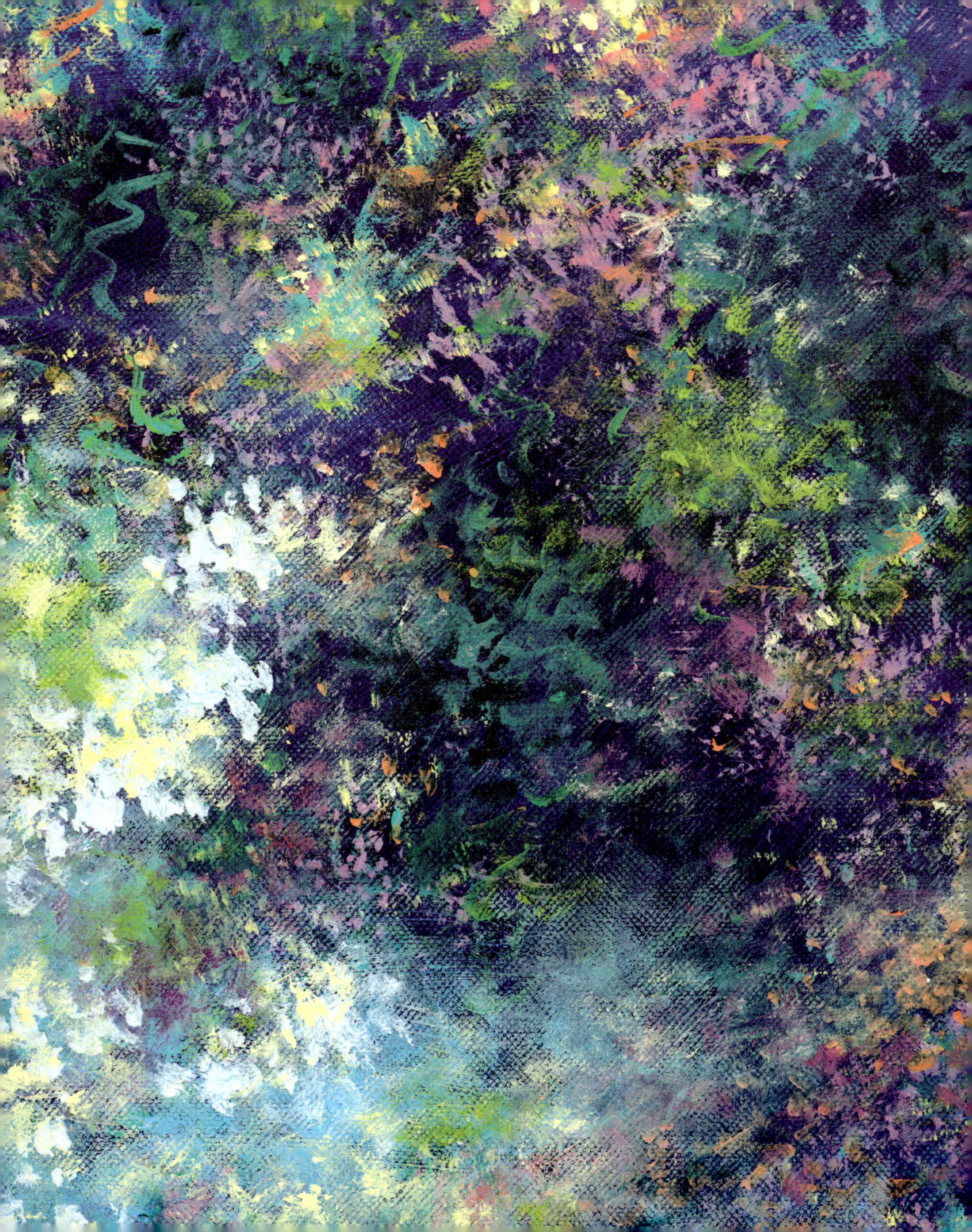

Watch the leaves dance and sing

With the joy of God's laughter

Watch the leaves dance and sing

With God's abundant good pleasure

Watch the leaves dance and sing forever and ever

For God has filled the leaves

With His Love without measure

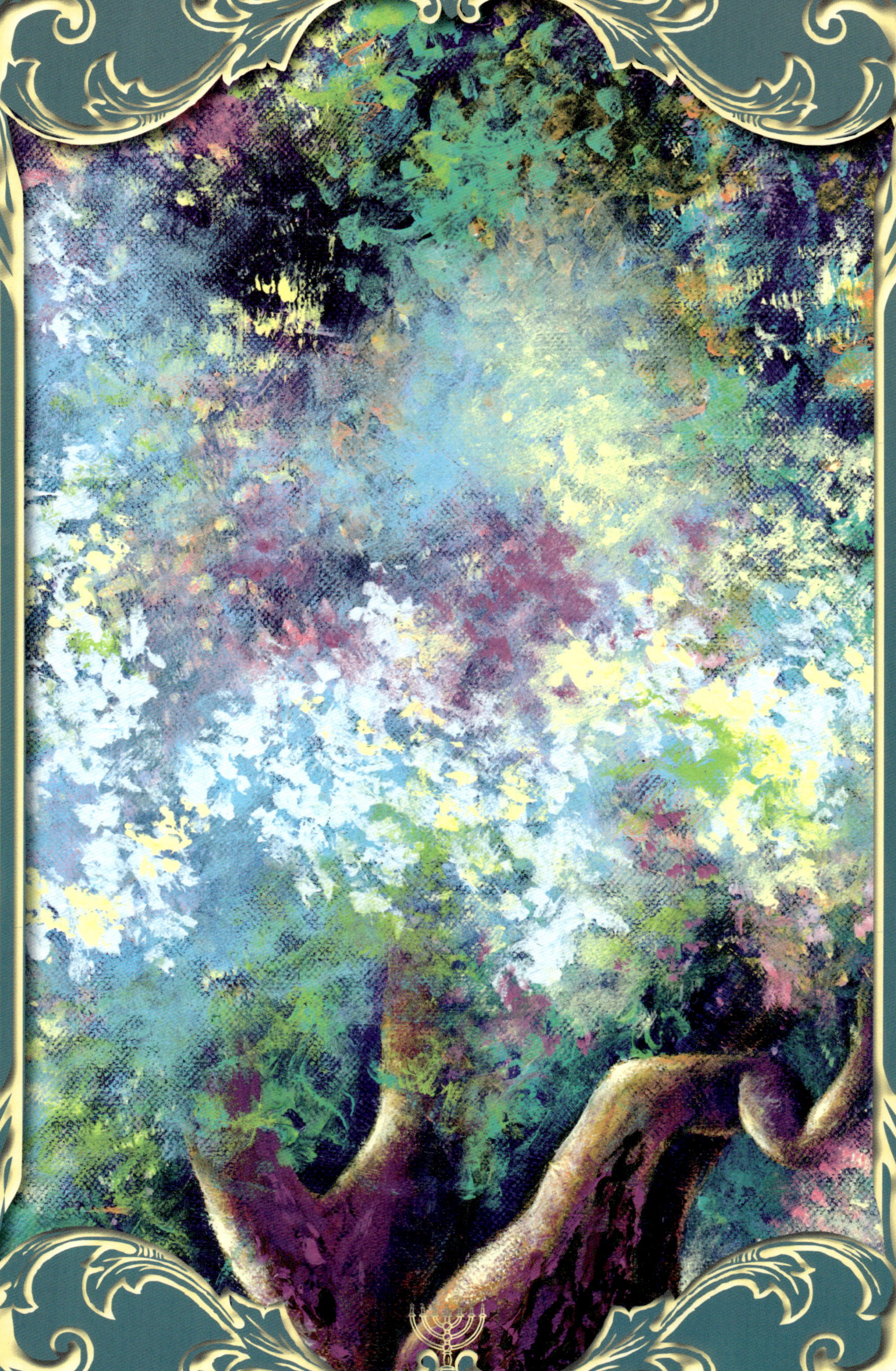

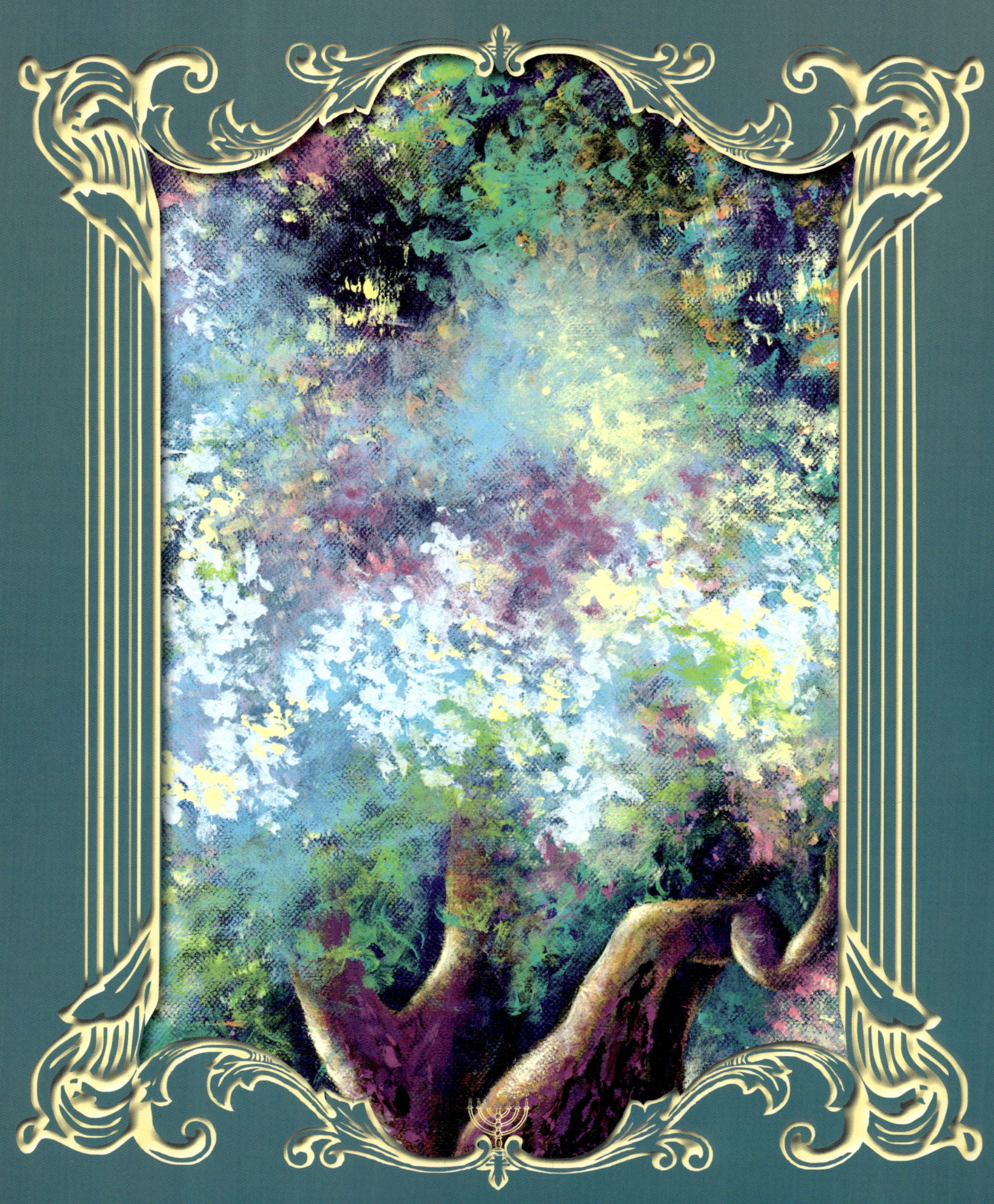

Becoming The One

You are the Joy set before Yeshua at the cross. You are the Glory set before Him at His death. Your intimacy with the Father is priceless. Practice His Presence. Practice His Freedom. Practice worship. Practice joy. It's like breathing. As you breathe shalom in, you breathe celebration out. In heaven, we will both worship the LORD and sit silently, in deep peace, before Him. As we proclaim, "Thy will be done, on earth, as it is in heaven," we are committing to live that rhythm now.

The rhythm is important to God. He follows it Himself. In Isaiah 55, after bringing His Saving Peace to Israel, He celebrates. He is so exultant, He even causes nature to sing and dance before her. Israel means "the power of God." When God is the power in your life, when God has filled you with His Saving Shalom, He celebrates you. He causes the mountains and the hills to sing before you, the trees to clap their hands for you. He sends you out with joy, and leads you forth with shalom. (Is 55:11-12)

Can we live a life composed entirely of peace and worship, of shalom and praise, of heaven on earth? I believe so. I believe it's time, and it's possible. When troubles surface, we can remember GOD'S Power. Everything is finished! We can respond to all circumstances, regardless of their origin, in God's peace and celebration. When He sends us out, we don't need to worry about anything. We are ripe, ready to fulfill our destinies, to love people no matter what, to be God's Light, to encourage people, to not judge them, to know the truth of Who God Is, and to help others discover it. In God, as long as we rest within His Peace, we are completely qualified. Our very lifeblood, the juice that flows through our veins, is the "Love of God." If we don't get distracted, if we don't let anything interfere with our awareness of that, God's creation itself will celebrate us. It yearns to do so. (Rom 8:18-25)

Contemplating The One

Because Yeshua accepted the cross, God's condition of peace for the world, Isaiah 55 is true. We know His rhythm of salvation. Calvary led to His death and His death led to His resurrection. We are each called to repeat that rhythm. His resurrection gives us the ability to pick up our crosses and bear them. "Yes" to the death of our "flesh" enables us to experience the peace of our surrender. Our peace causes us to rejoice with the LORD in His Victory over us. We become the perpetuating rhythm of salvation. We bring His salvation to others.

This happens only in Yeshua. In Him, mercy and faithfulness meet, righteousness and shalom kiss, truth springs up from the earth and righteousness looks down from heaven. (Ps 85:10-11) We become the betrothal of love and truth, of heaven and earth. We become the expression of God's Will being done, on earth as it is in heaven. Isaiah 9:7 promises us that "the increase of Yeshua's Shalom will never end." The increase of our shalom, in Him, is endless.

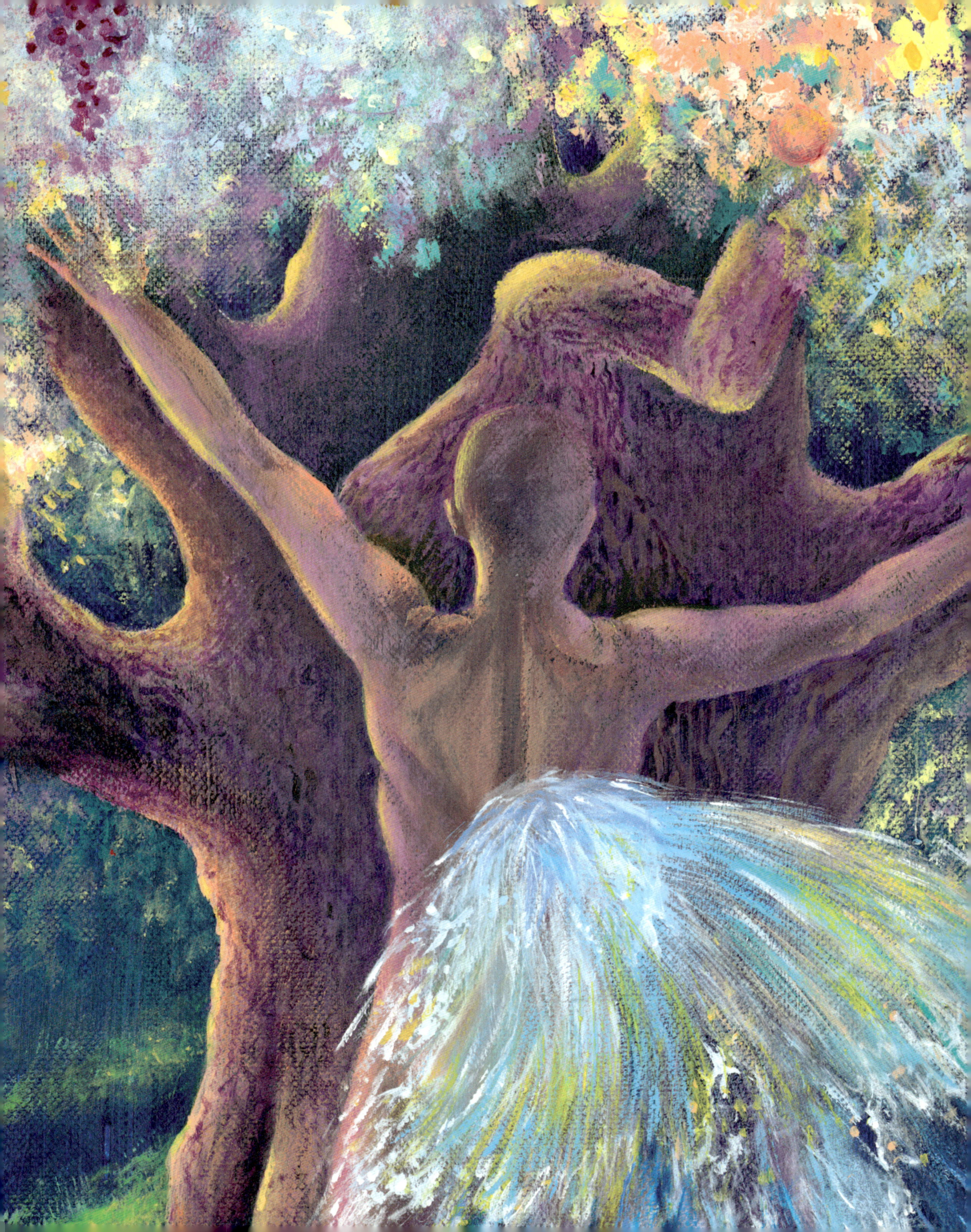

Drink deeply, my friend, of the Water of Life

Fill your roots with the truth from the Water of Life

Bring the Waters of Life

God's Spirit of Life

God's Spirit of Love

Into your own branches, into your own leaves

And let God's Spirit within you breathe

As God's fruit matures and ripens in you

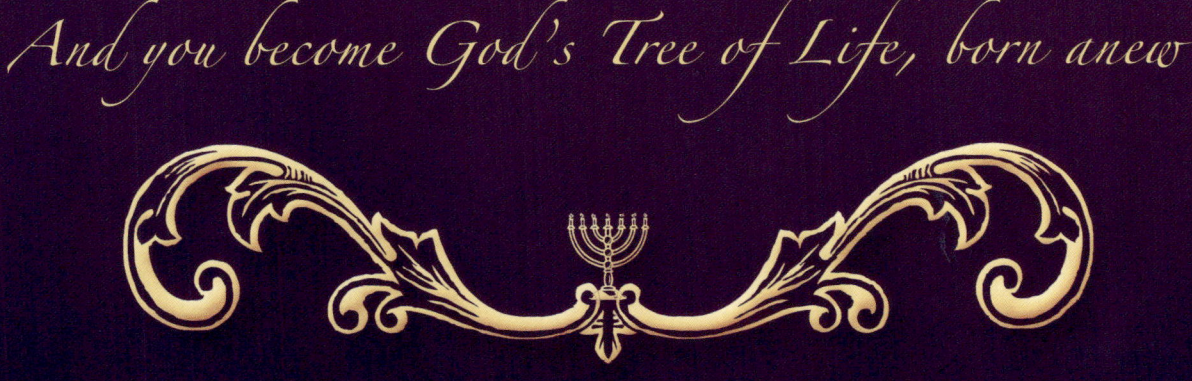

And you become God's Tree of Life, born anew

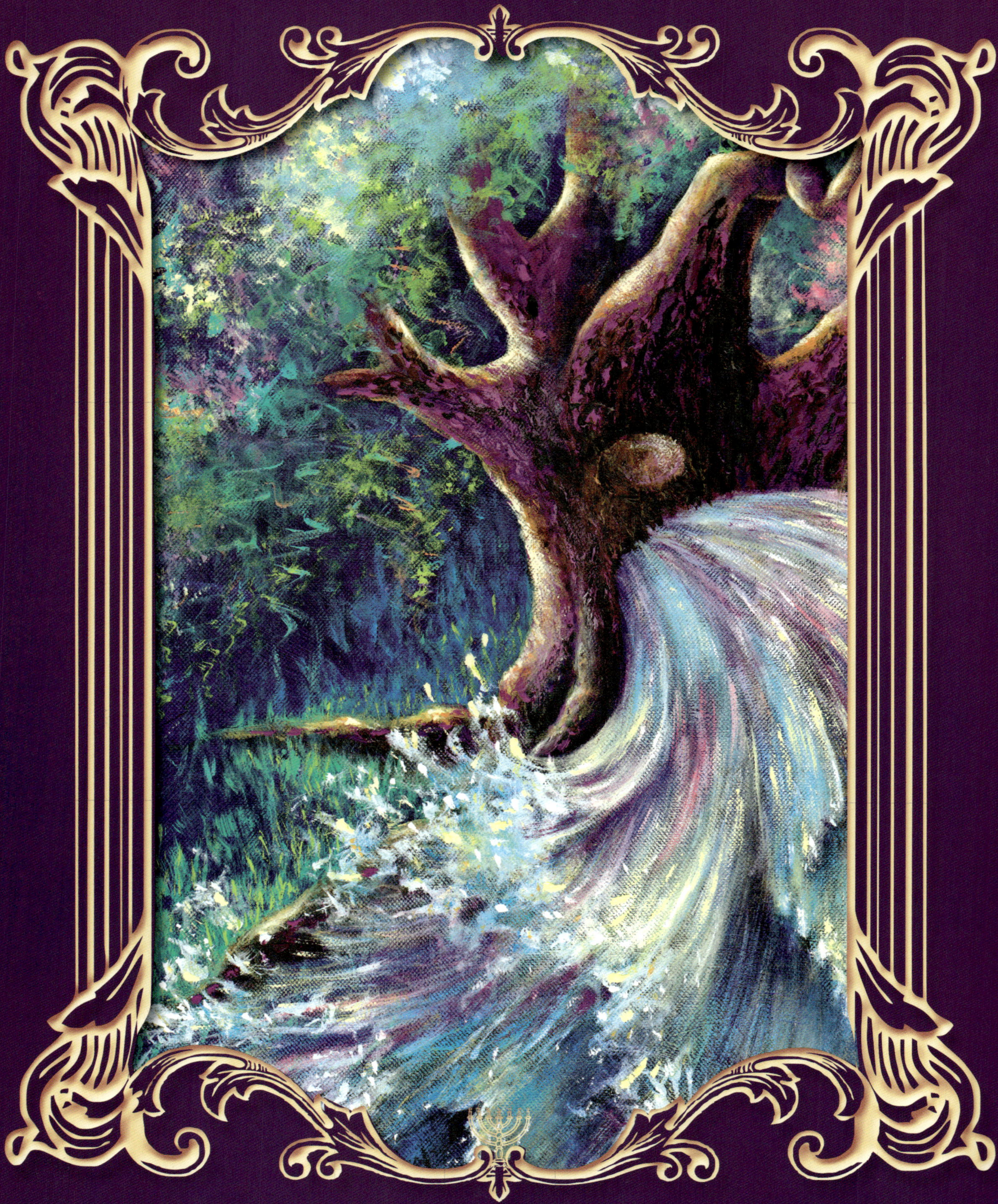

Becoming The One

God's love pours out through our bellies, touching people with His Mercy, the fullness of His Glory filling them through us. Because our most fragrant destined desire is to glorify the LORD, we delight in returning the entire honor to God, where it belongs. Because we exalt in His Goodness, we fall totally into His Spirit of Truth. Because God pours Himself thoroughly into our beings, we can dive to the bottom of His River, knowing we will live there for eternity. Because all that remains of us is His, we wait forever, deeply and quietly, reverently and worshipfully, upon God. Shouting and singing, dancing and proclaiming, we fill His River with our joy. The fact that "HE IS" becomes the fullness of all we know. Lost in Him, we are eternally found. Within His Embrace, our lives are penetratingly holy. We never leave His Arms of Grace. We know our lives are useless without His Staggeringly Brilliant Illuminated Face.

Dear LORD, it's time for me to live this fully from within Your Heart's Design, to allow the completion of Your Holy Will to become forever mine. Come, You who are my heart's desire, so I can be unified with Your Eternal Life. My spirit dissolves into Your Name, my soul releases its fragrance into Your Grace, and my body lives, on earth, within Your Holy Place. You are my compass, my path, my truth. You are holiness and unity renewed. My soul is sealed in Your Living Word. Now, I can release Your Fragrance to the world.

Dear LORD, thank YOU for bringing me to oneness with You, just as the incarnated Christ and You, Dear Father, were one. (John 17:21)

Contemplating The One

Think of anything you've wanted to do in life. It's Yeshua who gave you the ability to do it, it's Yeshua who gave you the ability to choose to do it, and it's Yeshua who gave you the ability to imagine yourself doing it. For instance, you have to choose to be in a race to win a race. But it's Yeshua who gave you the ability and the passion to run. You have to choose to get in a pool to swim. But it's Yeshua who gave you the imagination to use your arms and legs for swimming. The ability to ride a bike may rest fully within you, but you can't manifest that ability till you get on a bike and ride. It's a both/and.

Drinking of God's Spirit requires total commitment. It requires great tenacity. Total submersion into God's Goodness requires every bit of self-control we have. It also requires our complete let-go into God's Authority. It's a both/and. When Ruth went with Naomi, nothing could stop her. (Ruth 1:18) But to receive her redeemer, her Boaz, she had to trust him and sleep at his feet, resting under his robe. When Yeshua went to the cross, He set His Face like flint. Nothing could stop Him. But to receive His redeemed, His church, He had to trust God with His own murder, sleep in the dust, and rest under a burial shroud. The list goes on. Gideon. Joshua. Hezekiah… Strength. Determination. Trust. Submission. These are the hallmarks of the great leaders in Scripture. These need to be our hallmarks too.

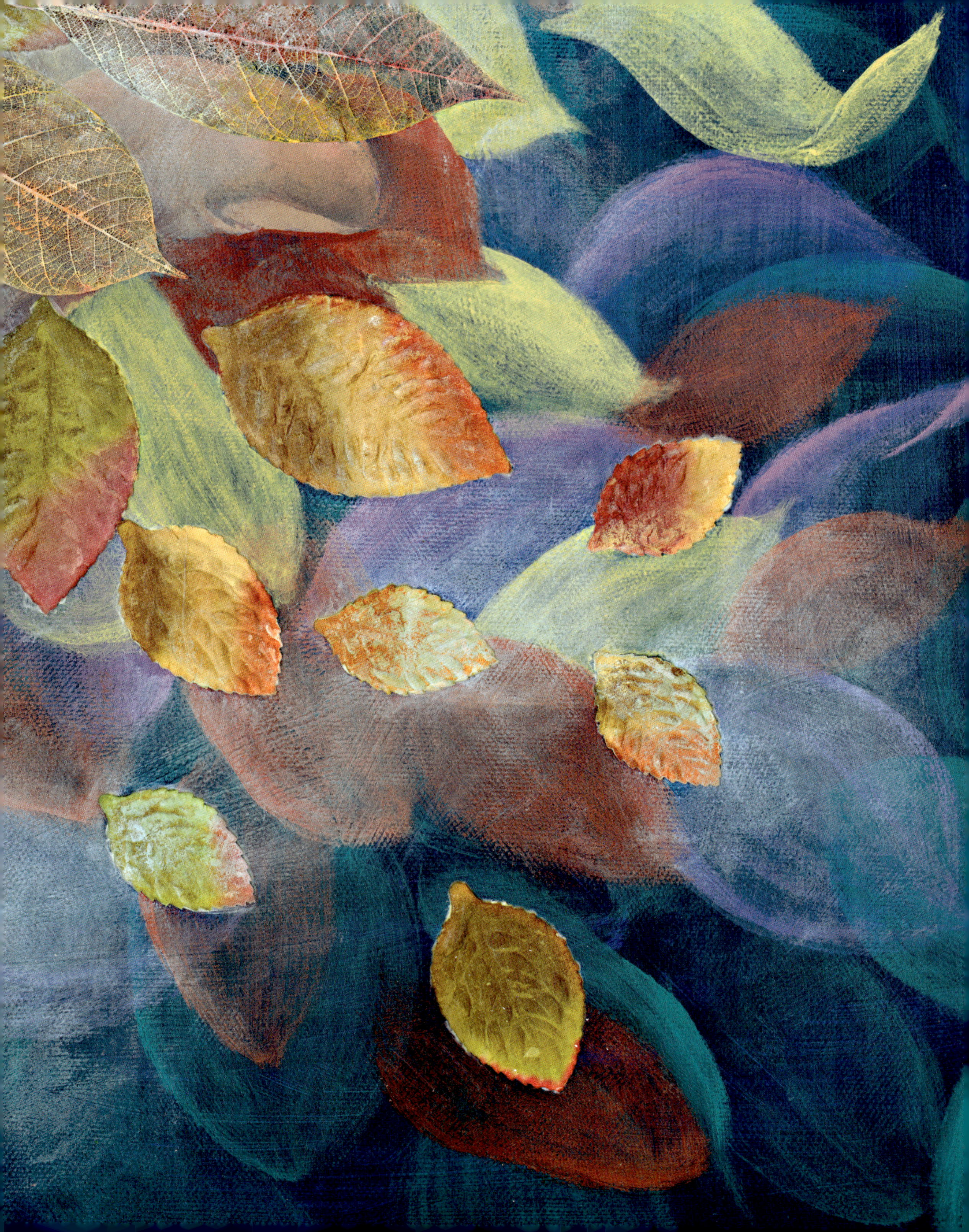

Now your leaves

Can provide shelter and shade

From all the troubles and the problems we face

Now your leaves

Can provide balm for our wounds

Healing our pain while their beauty renews

58

Becoming The One

The more we allow God to have His Will with us, the more we allow God to renew and revive us, the more love, peace, healing and joy we offer the world. The strength of our commitment deeply influences our ability to bless. We are the fruit of God's Loins, the gift of His Womb, the fulfilled joy of His Passion. He wants us to receive Him completely into our flesh, into our bodies, as well as into our souls and our spirits. He wants us. He wants us: body, mind, soul and spirit. He wants us to heal the world through Him. He wants to heal the world through us. He wants us to heal the world through Him. He wants us to choose Him over ourselves.

When we stand with Him, when we become His outreach, our faces must be set towards His Love like flint. Then, our commitment allows others to live, moment by moment, within the fullness of His Provision. When our hearts have been pierced through by His Sword, others, encountering us, can embrace their truth: they are all Yeshua's Beloved. When we impart blessings from within His Shalom, they can rest, alert and alive to His every breath. When we are rooted in our faith, they can stretch out further, reach out further, touch more people with His Love than ever before. Because God has entrusted us with the invisible, deeply centered, penetrating parts of ourselves that have never wavered from His Hand, we can comfort, protect, heal and inspire.

Let's imagine the LORD's triumphant shout… "YES! I went to the cross for the JOY set before me! For the Glory set before me! I knew My death upon the cross would give you the freedom to just BE in My Father. Nothing should stop your love and your joy and your satisfaction. Nothing. Not even the worst problems in life should interfere with your love of My Presence. Practice My Presence. Practice Patience. Practice Compassion. Practice Forgiveness. Practice Mercy. It's time. When problems surface, when they start, you will be prepared to heal them with My Love and Joy and Satisfaction."

Contemplating The One

God's highest judgment is Love. Yeshua is Healing Love in human skin, He is God's Agape judgment. He continuously shows us the healings effects of unconditional love. When He saved and forgave the adulterous woman, she sinned no more. (John 8:1-8) After He forgave Peter for denying Him, Peter began the early church. When the woman with five husbands encountered Yeshua, she brought her community to Messiah. (John 4) In the parable of the prodigal son, his father welcomed him with extravagant love, and completely restored him to his former position. Home. Salvation. Repentance. Deliverance. Freedom. Humility. Compassion. Joy. Resurrection. These are the results of God's ultimate judgment, God's healing love judgment. This is what we, God's trees of righteousness, are commissioned to give the world. What "the world needs now is love, sweet love. That's the only thing that there's just too little of." (Jackie DeShannon) That's us.

> "BY THE RIVER ON ITS BANK, ON ONE SIDE AND ON THE OTHER, WILL GROW ALL TREES FOR FOOD. THEIR LEAVES WILL NOT WITHER AND THEIR FRUIT WILL NOT FAIL. THEY WILL BEAR EVERY MONTH BECAUSE THEIR WATER FLOWS FROM THE SANCTUARY, AND THEIR FRUIT WILL BE FOR FOOD AND THEIR LEAVES FOR HEALING." (Eze 47:12)

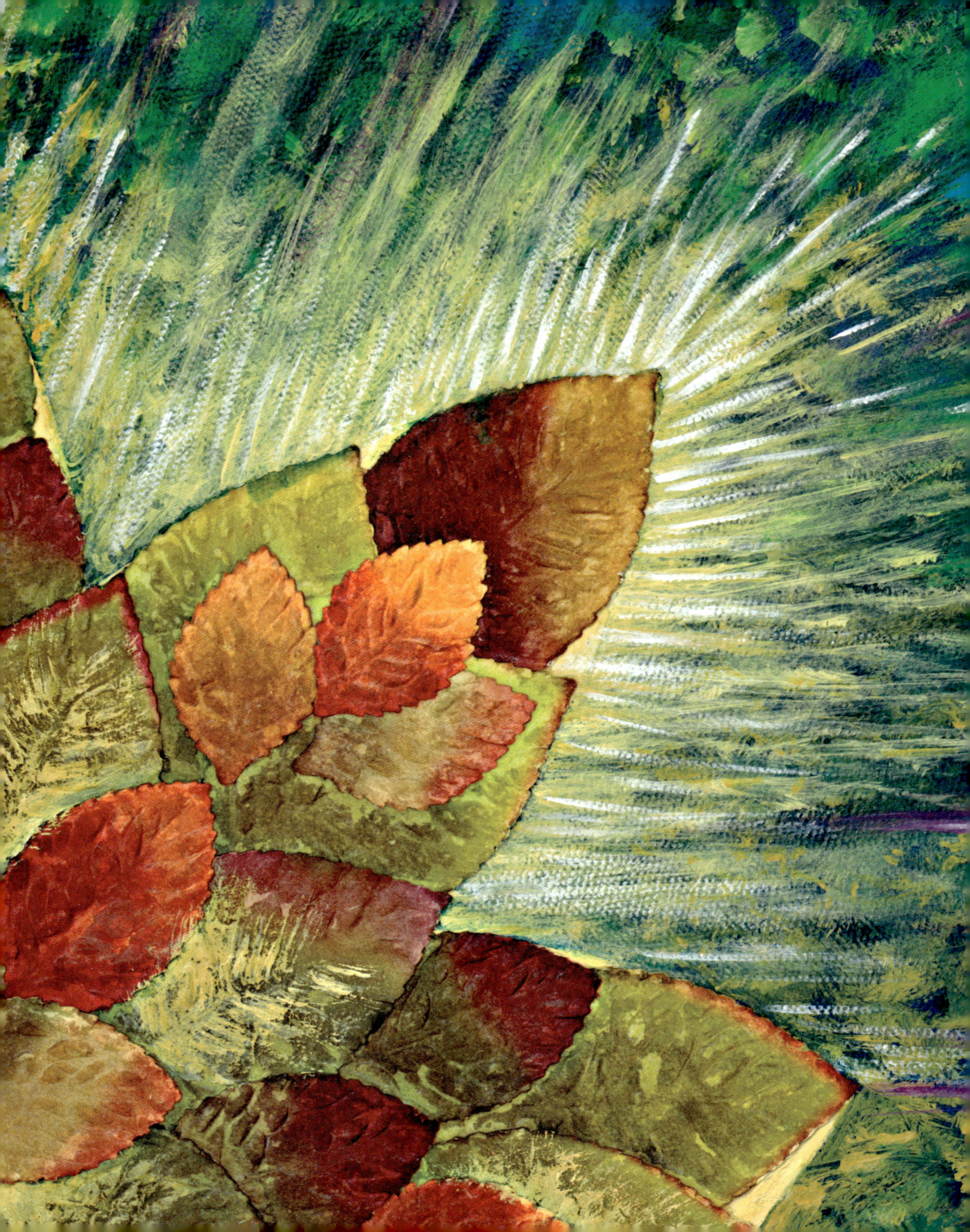

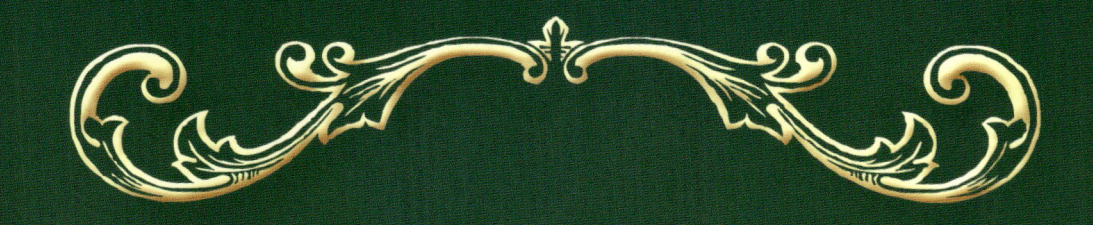

Now your leaves stretch out to the sun

They nourish your tree with the light of God's love

The light of God's love flows

Down through your leaves

Down through your branches

Down through your trunk, descending

Down through your roots

Back into God's eternal river of love

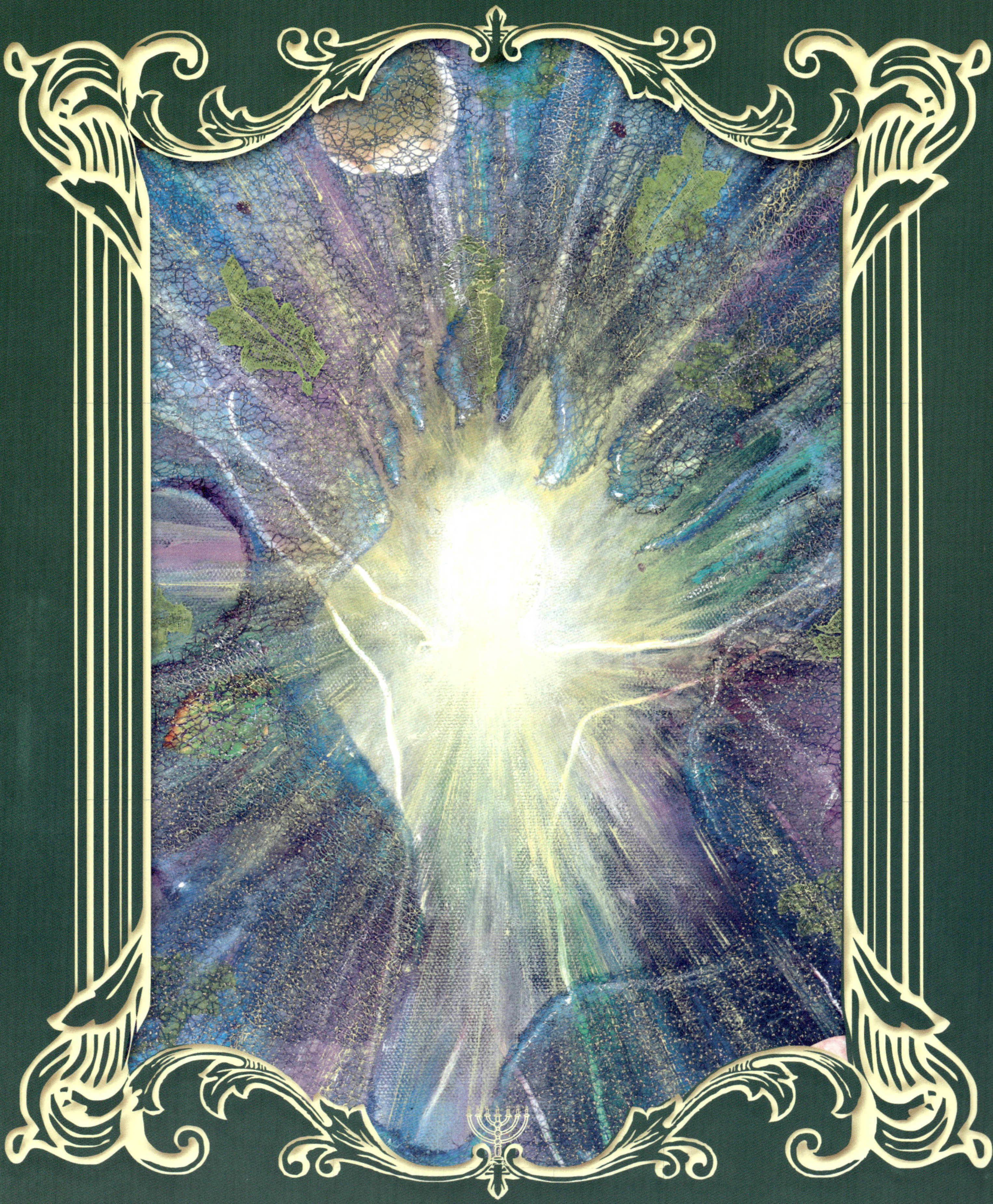

Becoming The One

Through us, God shows others their beauty. When we shed our self-made identities to become God's identity within us, we become God's Heart to the world, ambassadors of His Name. Like Sha'ul/Paul on the Damascus road, our vision becomes profoundly transformed, causing us to become totally indebted to Yeshua. We can do nothing but serve Him. Like Nebuchadnezzar, we regain our sanity and can only praise God. Like Moses at the Burning Bush, God's commissioning consumes our days and nights. We are the fruit of His loins, the celebrated gift of His womb, the fulfilled joy of His passion. We are healthy. Our fingertips bring His Touch to the world, and His Touch is wholeness. God's Love heals people through us, bringing forth the ripeness of His Ravishing Goodness within them.

God's glorious desire is to bring wholeness of wellness, heaven on earth, to those who love Him, who are called according to His Name. Whether He works through peace or tumult, He creates a tapestry of extraordinary beauty. All of His actions are purposed to bring healing to the nations and health to the world. There is no greater privilege, on earth, than to serve Him.

> Dear Yeshua, May I serve You well. Root my soul and my spirit in Your Love. Fill my mind and my heart with Your Waters. Give me hands of healing love for the world. Complete Yourself, dear LORD, within me. Amen.

Contemplating The One

Faith and truth are the same noun in Hebrew, emunah. The participle for emunah is amen, which means "to be faithful." The root meaning of emunah is to carry and support a child, to raise it well. This is how God raises us. He teaches us truth through His faithfulness. He carries us when we are newborns. He supports us as we grow. He matures us till we are beautiful kings and queens of truth who demonstrate His faithfulness in His Kingdom. Psalm 33:4 tells us that all YHWH's work is emunah. Deuteronomy 32:3-4 tells us that YHWH is a Rock of emunah. Yeshua said, "This is the work of God: believe in Him whom He has sent." (John 6:29) For then, rivers of living water will flow from our bellies. (John 7:38) Truth will flow from our guts. To believe in Yeshua is truth. It is our work. It is the Light that flows through us, that pours down into God's River and fills the world with His Peace. Choose to become that River, that Tree, that Light. Choose to become. Have faith in Him. Trust in His Word. Be beautiful.

He will do all He has promised. He will finish His Perfect Work. His Word will not return void. Be diligent. Anticipate His Goodness. Trust in His Strength. Commit to His Glory. Stand steadfast. Be tenacious. Be forbearing. Be resilient. Worship Him. Praise Him. The result is true, glorious life; bodies, souls and spirits filled with His Joy, Peace and Empowerment; days full of wonder and amazement; moments full of discovery and adventure, as God's Love heals people through you, bringing forth the ripeness of His Goodness within them.

> "UNLESS A GRAIN OF WHEAT FALLS INTO THE EARTH AND DIES, IT REMAINS ALONE; BUT IF IT DIES, IT BEARS MUCH FRUIT." (John 12:24)

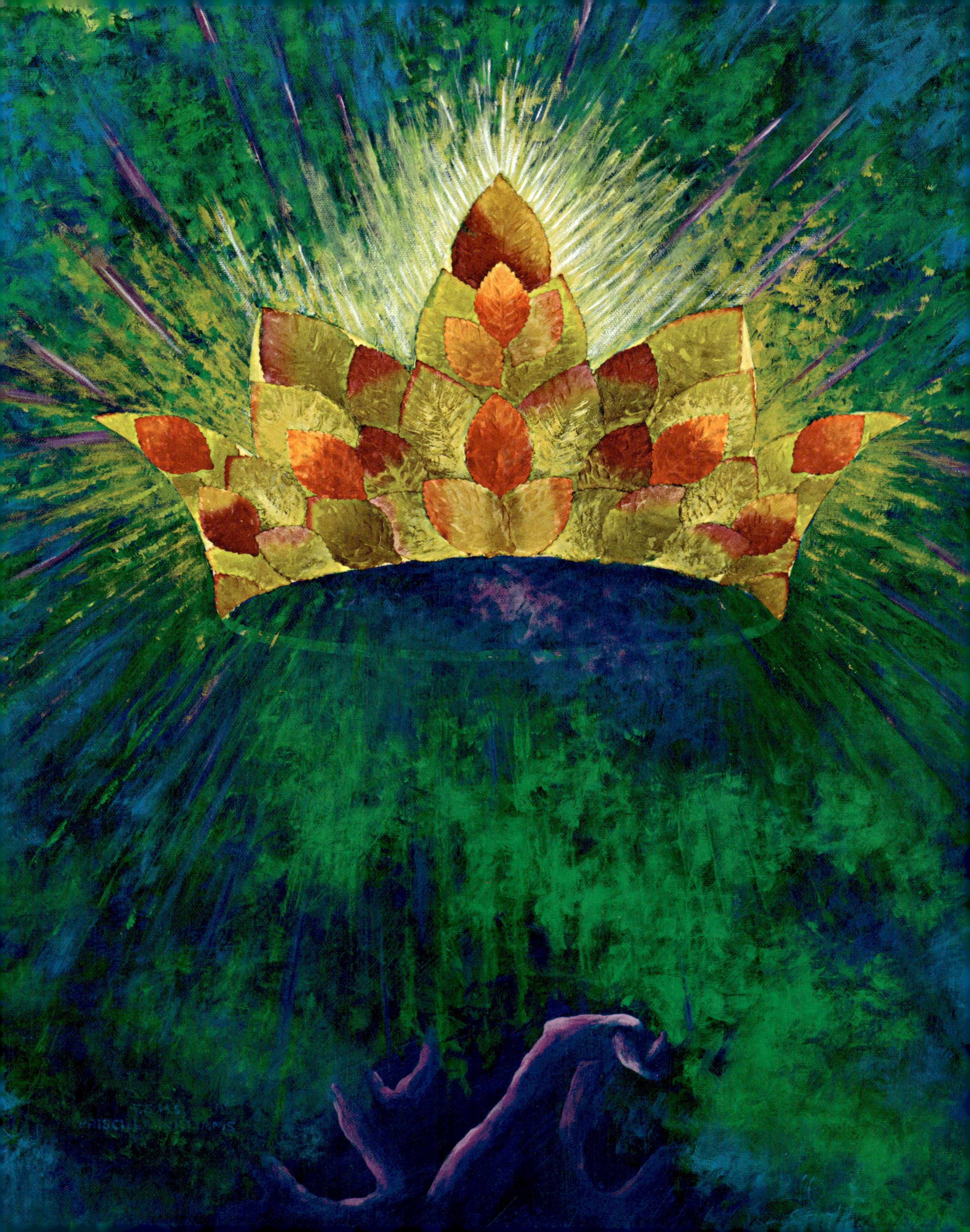

Your leaves are now

The most important part of your tree

For through their protection

And the solace they bring

The nations can rest

Enjoying God's beauty in peace

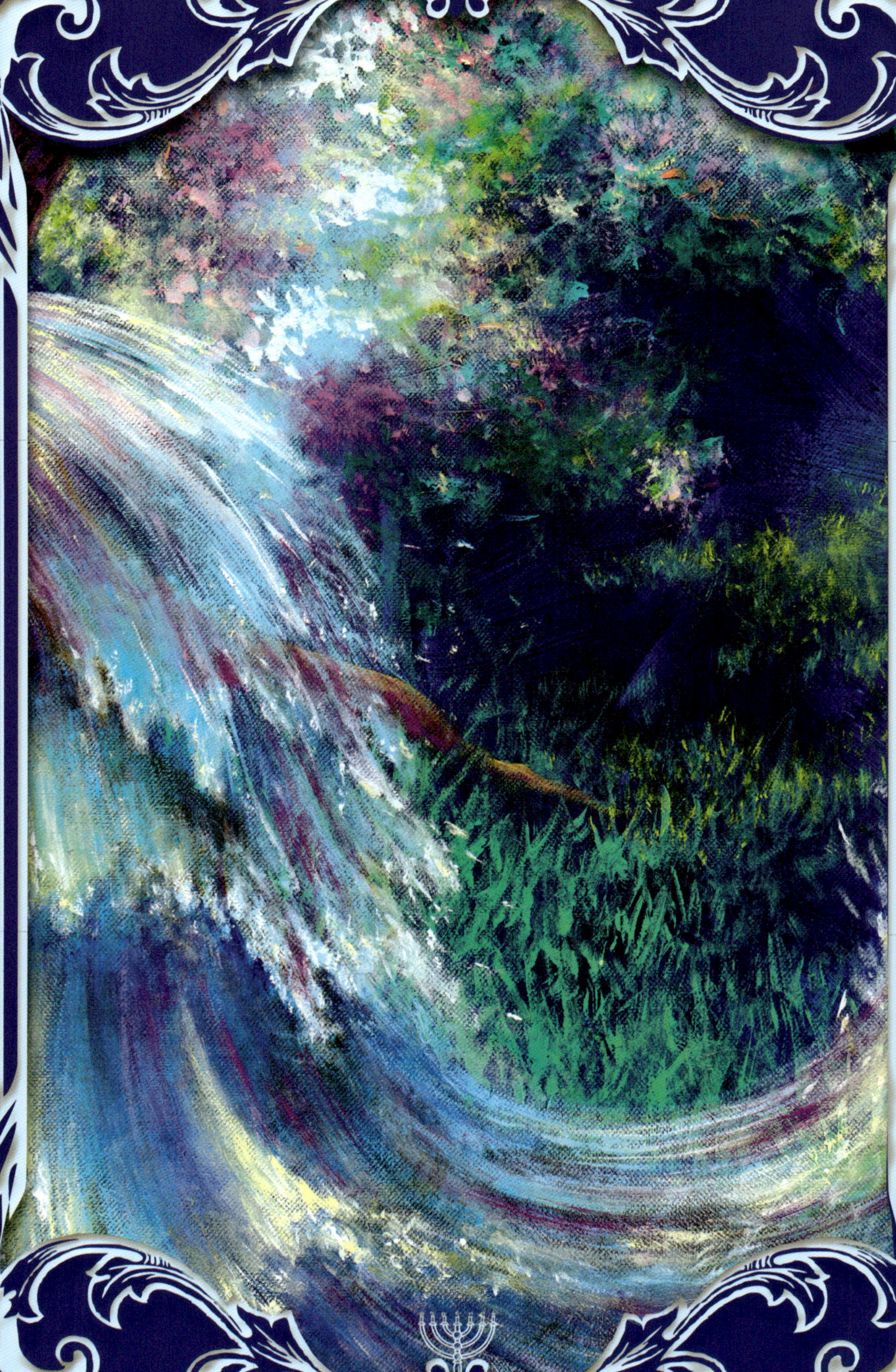

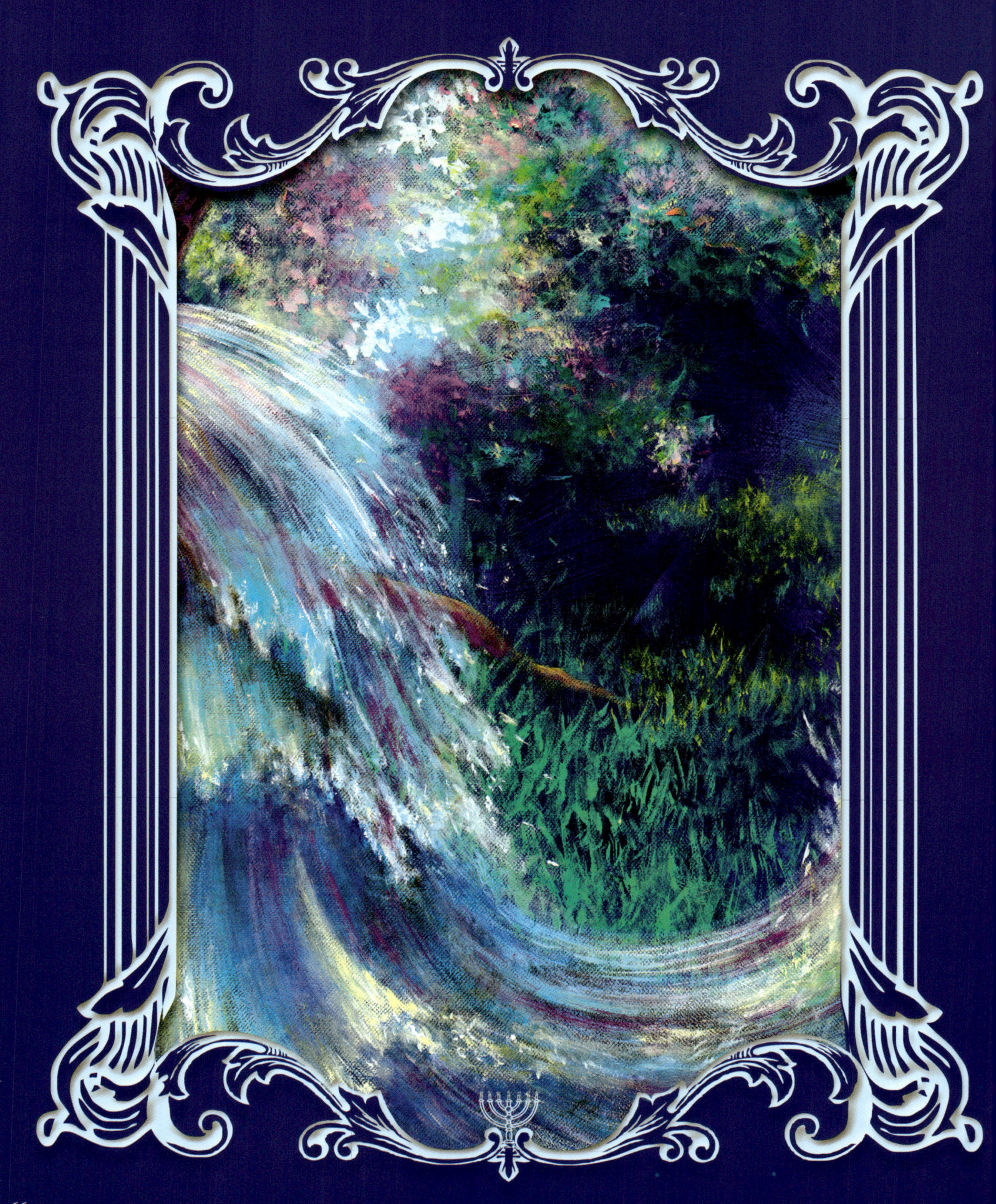

Becoming The One

God rejoices with those who rejoice and grieves with those who grieve. (Rom 12:15) Apprehending the Heart of God means apprehending both Yeshua's pain and joy. Joy is luscious and thrilling and wonderful, necessary food for our existence. But thank God, Yeshua embraces our hurts and pains. He embraces it all. To be His Arms of mercy, we must FEEL, as well as BE. Because some emotions hurt, we must stay deep inside Yeshua's Spirit of Compassion, of Merciful Goodness, and never get out of His River. Yeshua wailed over Jerusalem, (Matt 23) and He went to the cross for the joy set before Him. (Heb 12:2) He chose pain, sorrow and seeming defeat, as well as joy, pleasure and true victory, all for His Father's Glory. (John 17) Yeshua does not want to keep any part of Himself separate from us. He wants to cry and laugh into the world through us. Yeshua asks us into the fellowship of His suffering, as well as the glory of His resurrection. Without the pain of God's Heart, joy on earth sounds shrill. Without the joy of God's Heart, pain on earth sounds deafening. Within God's Presence, each and every emotion sounds harmonious. He carries them within us, and His burden is easy and His yoke is light. It is when we stop surrendering them to Him that we get stuck. Then, they become heavy.

When our touch is fully God's, our touch is pure, holy and wholesome. People can be safe with us, regardless of their condition. God can pour His Protective Truth, His Healing Comfort, through us to them. We can offer them His Love, Shalom, and Hope, without restriction or bias. We become His Arms of Rest, His Fingertips of Tender Love, and God can pour His Just, Restorative Goodness into the world through us. This happens fully when we choose the LORD with ALL our hearts, minds and souls, and are undivided in our devotion to Him. This is our commitment and our destiny. This is who we are now, in God's Heart, and this is who we are becoming…

Contemplating The One

Fellowship, meaning transparent, self-sacrificing, friendship and love, is a theme throughout Scripture. In the New Testament, the word "koinonea" (G2842) is used to describe this wonderful communion: fellowship amongst believers by breaking of bread and prayers, (Acts 2:42) fellowship with the poor by giving and sharing, (2 Cor 8:4; 9:13) fellowship with God's Son by recognizing God's faithfulness, (1 Cor 1:9) fellowship in the Gospel by knowing that God will complete what He started, (Phil 1:5-6) fellowship in the Spirit through love, unity and humility, (Phil 2:1-4) and fellowship with Messiah through communion. The most repeated reference to fellowship in Messiah is fellowship in His suffering and resurrection. As Paul says, "that I may know Him and the power of His resurrection and the fellowship of His sufferings, being conformed to His death in order that I may attain to the resurrection from the dead. (Phil 3:10-11)

"FOR WE, BEING MANY, ARE ONE BREAD AND ONE BODY, ALL PARTAKERS OF THAT ONE BREAD." (1 Cor 10:16-17)

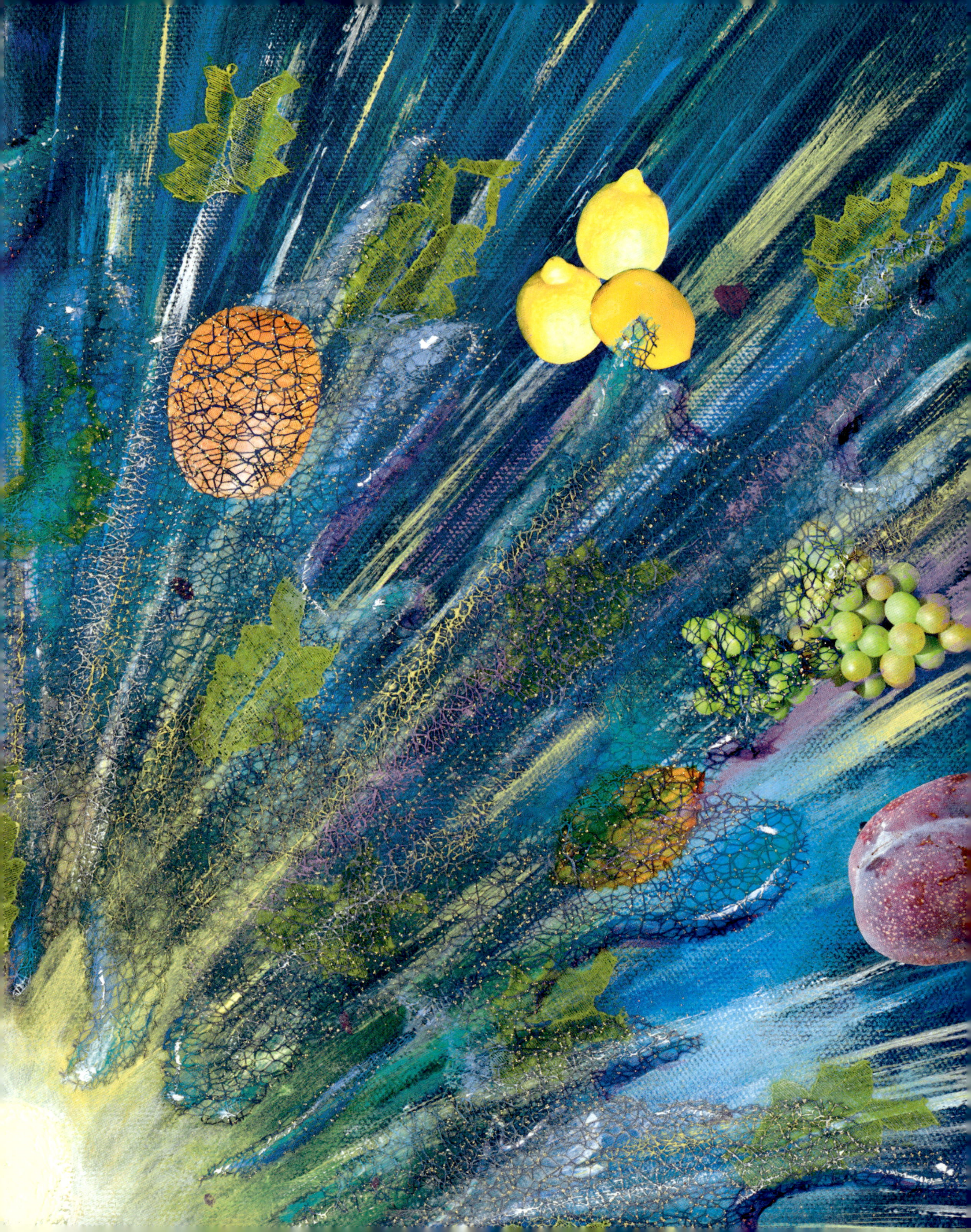

But it is God's fruit

My friend, that nourishes us all

Without its sustenance our

Faith might fall

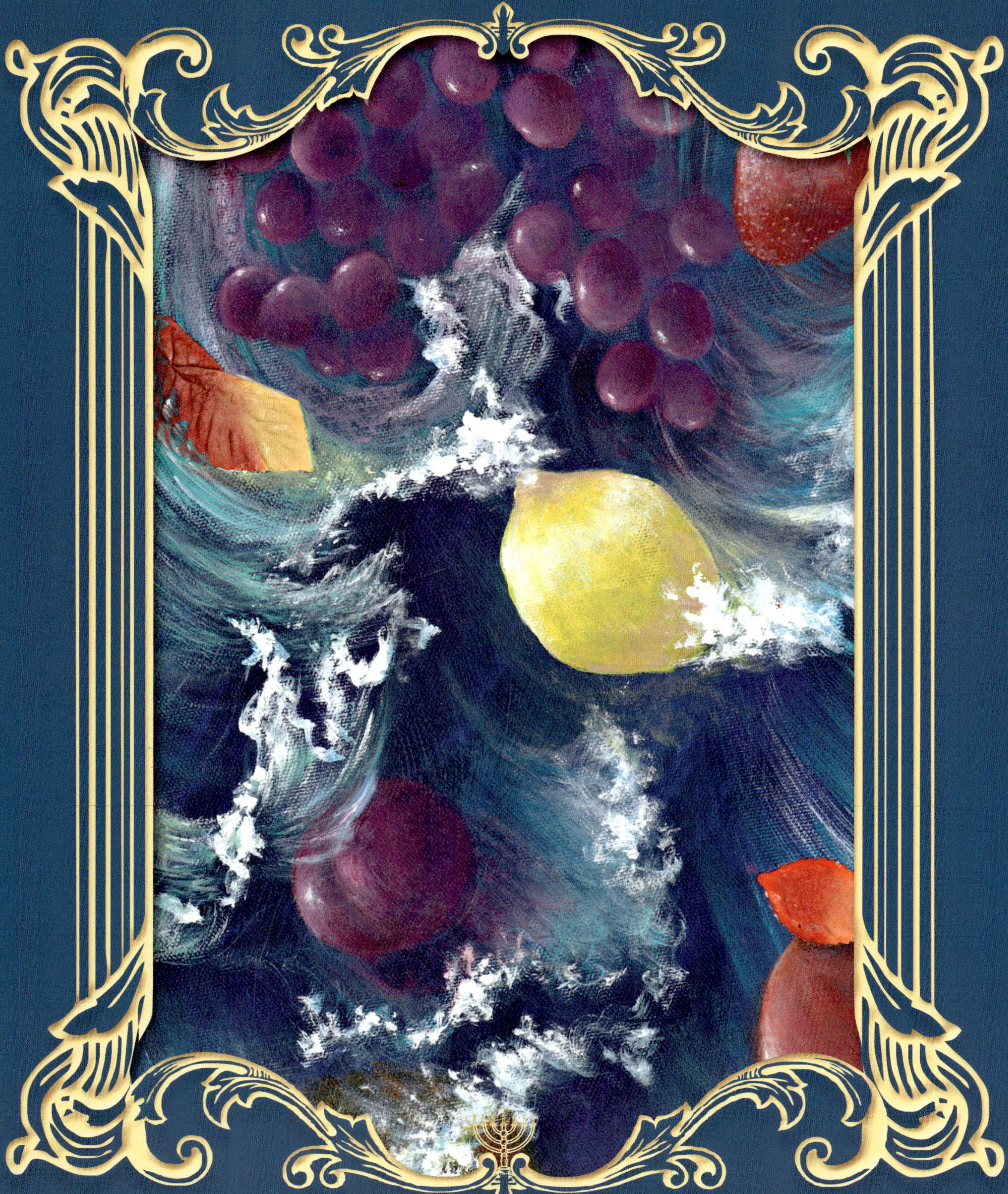

Becoming The One

Let us eat deeply from YHWH's Fruit until we are completely satisfied, till we want for nothing and need nothing. Let us let Him satiate us with His Love, transforming us into His Offering, into His Sacrifice, into His Goodness. Let us become YHWH's Fruit to THE WORLD. We will rest deeply, full of great activity, strength and power. We will function as priests, bringing each other's prayers to God. We will function as prophets, bringing God's blessings to each other. We will function as God's Ambassadors, bringing God's Fruit to the world. YHWH will help us to think, feel and say what will bear good fruit. He will teach us to keep our focus on Him.

Nothing else is needed. Nothing else is required. Our focus, our faith, is all that remains for us. At the cross, everything was finished. But our choice remains important. When everybody chooses to bring healing and blessing and encouragement to each other, everybody is careful to overshadow and comfort each other, and all become safe, ripe and ready to fulfill their destinies, to love people no matter what, to encourage them, to know the truth of YHWH and help others find it. When the Body of Messiah desires this sufficiently, we will all experience the totality of His Fullness dwelling amongst us. We will know His Face. When everybody does that for everybody else, we will bring YHWH's healing and blessing to the entire world.

Contemplating The One

Dear LORD, Oh, how Your Spirit loves me! You bring me joy and fill me with peace. You have patience with my shortcomings and show me unending kindness. You, the most Faithful Friend imaginable, only bring good into my life. You are gentle with me and control Your Emotions when I lose mine. Thank You for the wholesome, refreshing and life giving fruit of Your Spirit. Because of You, I will bear much fruit. Because of You, I can bring Your Fruit to the world. (Gal 5:22-23)

Yes, Dear LORD, because of Your Holiness, I can fulfill Your Great Commission. I can go and bear eternally good fruit. I can bear holy fruit that will last. I can ask the Father for whatever I need, in Your Name, and He will give it to me. Because of Your Love, I can obey Your Command to love all others. (John 15:16-17) Because of Your Goodness, I will bring Your goodness to the world.

But, Dear YHWH, I need to be more thoroughly cleansed to do this well. Take everything from me that bears no fruit and prune the rest. Destroy everything within me that stands in Your Way, now and forever. (John 15:2) I pray to be Your Radiant Seed, Your Nourishing Holiness, Your Taste of Heaven on Earth. In Yeshua's Holy Name, I pray. Amen and amen.

"HE WHO DOES NOT TAKE HIS CROSS AND FOLLOW AFTER ME IS NOT WORTHY OF ME. HE WHO HAS FOUND HIS LIFE WILL LOSE IT, AND HE WHO HAS LOST HIS LIFE FOR MY SAKE WILL FIND IT." (Matt 10:38-39)

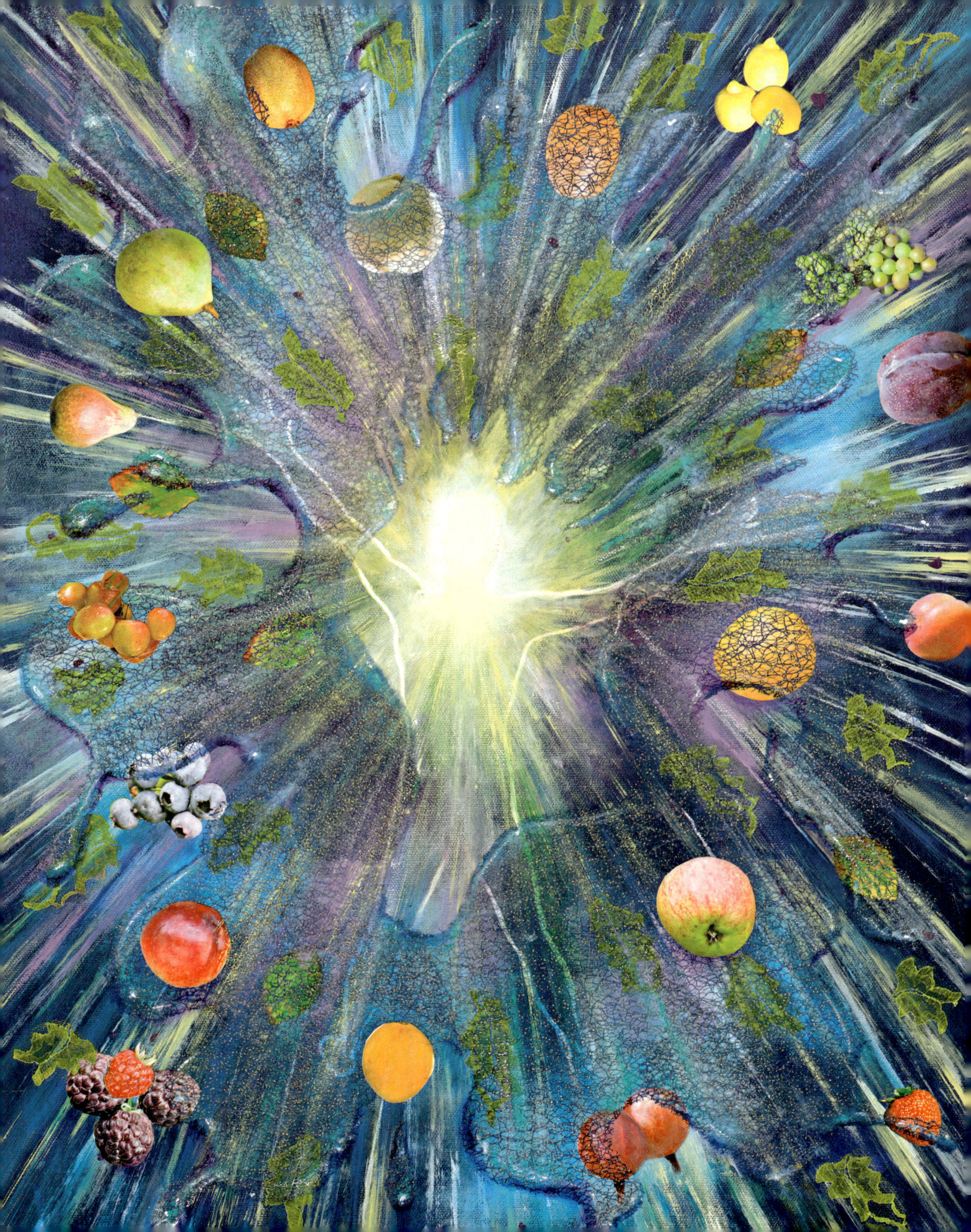

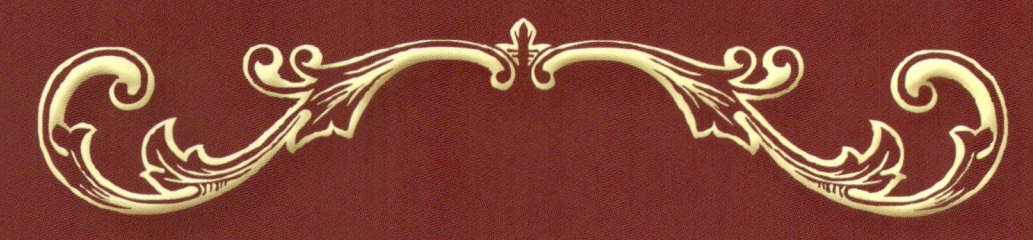

So God says dive deep

Dive deeper still

Until you are drunk and totally filled

With the joy of His presence

The desire for His fruit

And all you crave are

His waters of truth

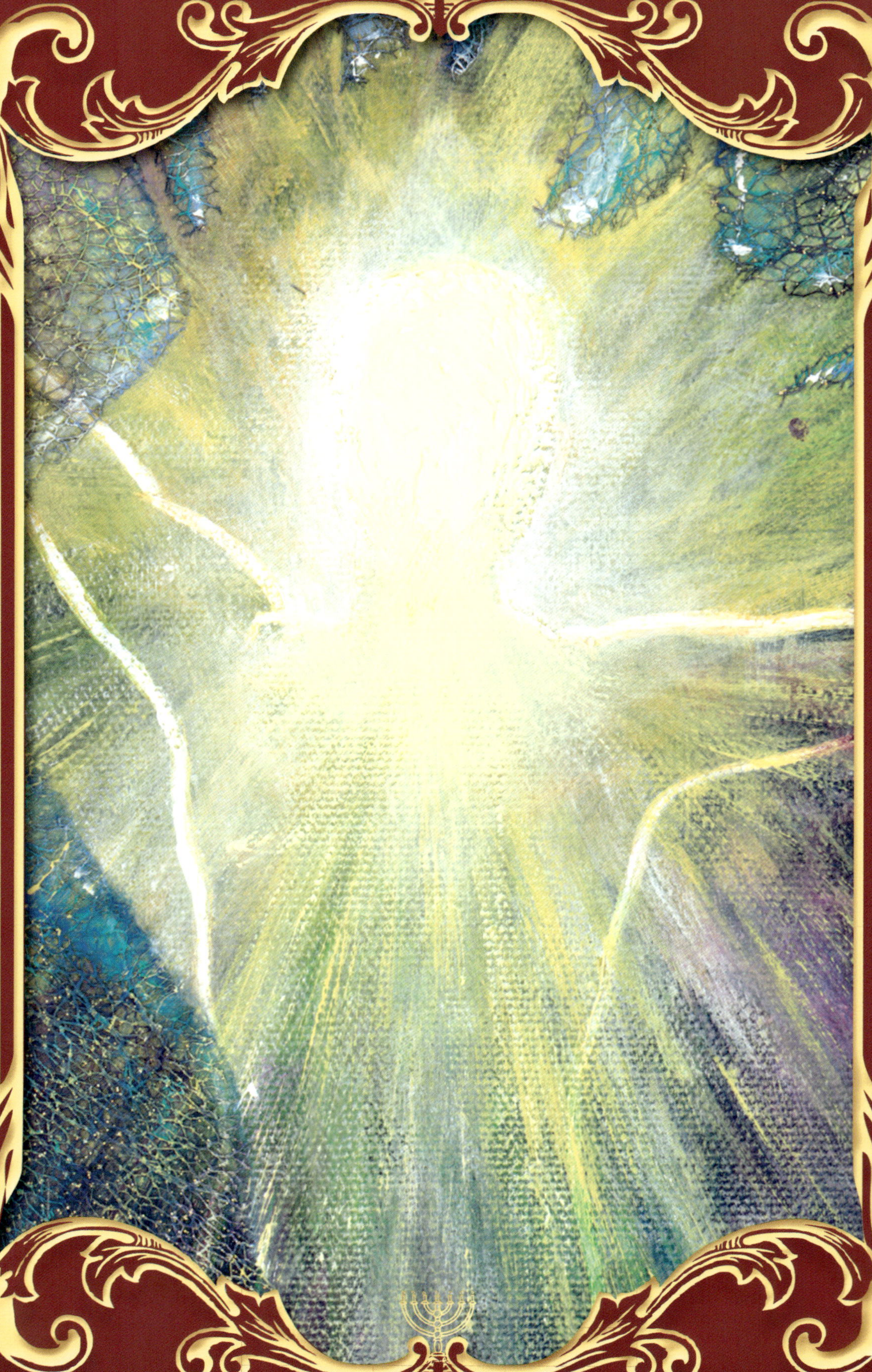

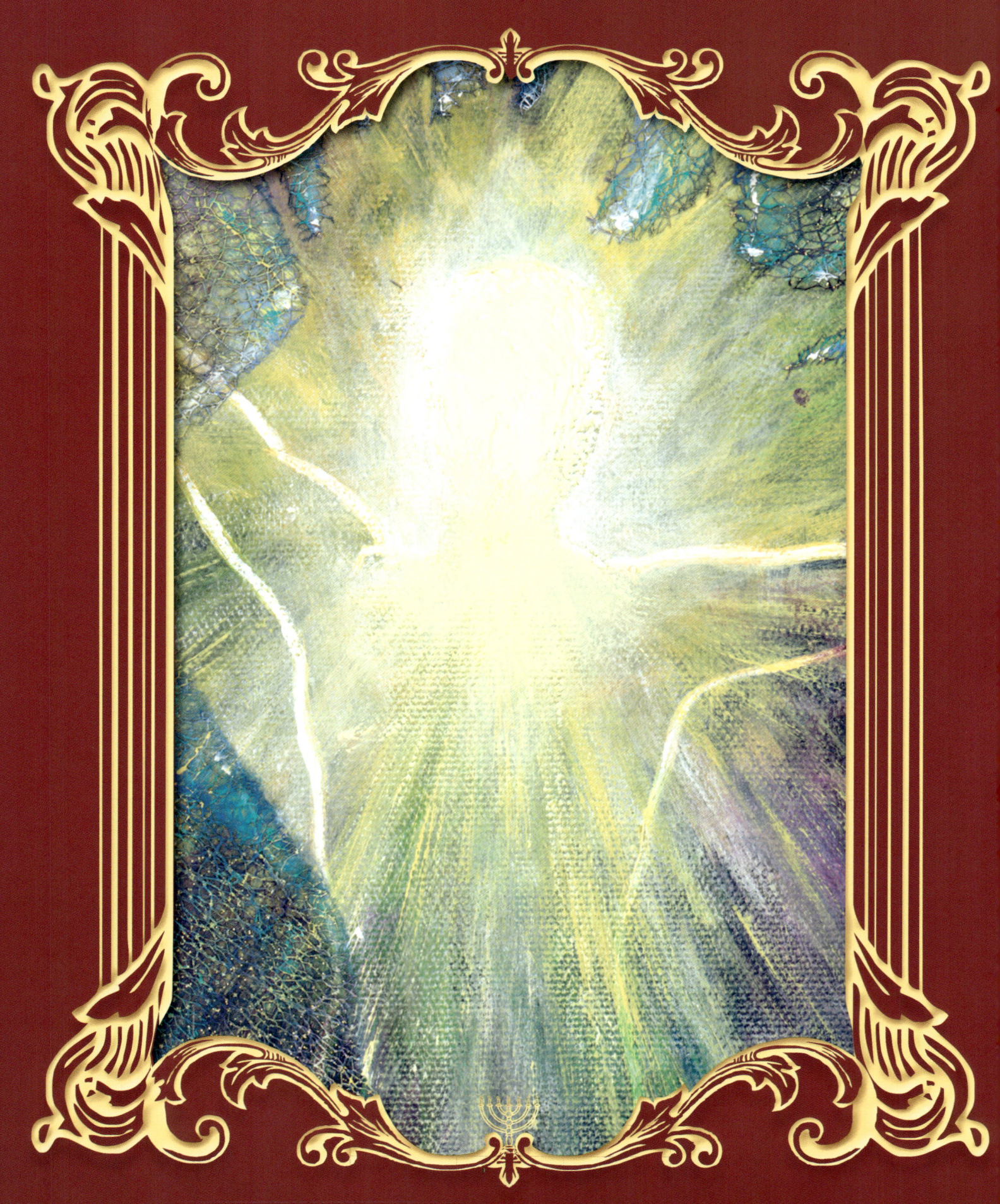

Becoming The One

The joy of God's Presence in our lives is profoundly rich. When we dive totally into His Pleasure, He can make us giddy with delight. We can wander through our days immersed in satisfaction, each and every iota of God's Creativity delighting us. But the depth of the painfulness of life is also profound, and we need to learn to be safe in the LORD, regardless of the strength of our emotions and heartbreak. To the extent that we respond emotionally in the LORD, we can live and heal. To the extent that we feel, we can reach others with God's Compassion, and they can heal. It matters that we are willing to embrace and care for those we meet. It matters, costs, and gives. When we reach the point where we are willing to feel anything, we have peace. When we can dive into the vast depths of Yeshua's River, handing Him all our tumult, we discover His Joy and His Mercy. When we ignore what we are feeling, we die.

Eagles' wings await us. With them, we can soar to heaven and descend to the depths of the earth. Under the covering of His Wings, every single emotion can become holy and life giving. With God, what we have in each other can be beyond compare. We can go to unimaginably good places, experience incomprehensibly tender mercy, and become compassionately happy beyond our conception. We can become reservoirs for God's Love in all circumstances.

> Dear LORD, You have called me to be Your Hands, Your Arms of Embrace, Your Touch to the world. I say "yes" to Your Love Call upon my life. I choose to pay Your price forever. Your price is Love. Your reward is Love. Your Call is Love. I choose Love, Your Love, above all else, over and over and over and over again. I choose to never make another choice. I am ready!

Contemplating The One

When God gave Joshua the Promised Land, God did not offer him a "walk in the park," but a promise that he would win every battle and conquer every inch of the territory, as long as he and the Israelites remained clean in heart and deed. God told him, "EVERY PLACE YOU STEP WITH THE SOLE OF YOUR FOOT, I AM GIVING TO YOU … NO MAN WILL STAND AGAINST YOU ALL THE DAYS OF YOUR LIFE … I WILL NOT FAIL YOU OR FORSAKE YOU." (Josh 1:2-5) Similarly, when Yeshua won the victory upon the cross and gave us His Spirit, we received our territory: heaven on earth. We get the spoils of victory: to preach the Good News, destroy the enemy's power, see salvations, and experience the Glory of God's Kingdom on earth. We get to bring the Gospel to the afflicted, bind up the brokenhearted, proclaim liberty to captives, open the prisons of those who are bound, declare the favorable year of the Lord, comfort all who mourn, give them a garland instead of ashes, the oil of gladness instead of mourning, and the mantle of praise instead of a spirit of fainting, so they will be called oaks of righteousness, the planting of the Lord, that He may be glorified! (Is 61:1-3) We get to be God's vessels of grace. Alleluiah! Let's go conquer some territory!

Blossom, ripen

Be born anew

Feel your tree groan and shake

With the weight of your fruit

Be nourished by others

And nourishment be

As we learn to become

Fruit in God's Tree